Beyond a House Divided

Beyond a House Divided

The Moral Consensus Ignored
by Washington, Wall Street,
and the Media

Carl Anderson

Doubleday

New York   London   Toronto   Sydney   Auckland

DD

DOUBLEDAY

Published in the United States by Doubleday Religion, an imprint of
the Crown Publishing Group, a division of Random House, Inc., New York.
www.crownpublishing.com

DOUBLEDAY and the DD colophon are registered trademarks
of Random House, Inc.

Library of Congress Cataloging-in-Publication Data is available upon request.

ISBN 978-0-307-88774-0

Printed in the United States of America

10 9 8 7 6 5 4 3 2 1

First Edition

Contents

Acknowledgments   7

Foreword   9

1   Beyond a House Divided: Our Moral Compass   15

2   Beyond the Wall of Separation: Religion in America   27

3   Beyond Greed: Toward Morality in the Marketplace   43

4   Beyond Partisan Politics: Values-based Leadership   61

5   Beyond the Clash of Absolutes: Abortion   79

6   Beyond Mythology: The Statistics on Marriage   97

7   Beyond Red and Blue:
    What We Can Do for Our Country   119

Notes   131

Acknowledgments

Behind every book is a story—a story of the countless people whose suggestions, ideas, research and hard work helped shape the author's ideas and words into the fruit of that labor you now hold in your hands. This book was shaped by the work of many whose input proved invaluable.

There are instances in life when a few words can have great meaning; finding the survey questions that are able to take the pulse of Americans' values are just such instances. I am deeply grateful to Lee Miringoff and Barbara Carvalho and their team at the Marist Institute for Public Opinion, who lent their expertise and time to this project, helping bring all of us a clearer picture of who we are as Americans. Their experience and contributions were vital from beginning to end, as it has been in our cooperative work on creating the "Moral Compass Project," 2008, a mutual effort that laid the foundations for, and shed light on, the many issues covered in this book. Barbara was especially helpful in guiding us through the data from our latest poll—completed in late July 2010—just weeks before the manuscript was due.

Trying to discover what Americans actually think on so many issues—through our own polling and the other survey data available—was a massive undertaking. It could not have been accomplished without the able research staff members at the Knights of Columbus who were invaluable for their research ability and insights, and indefatigable in their work ethic. It took many long days and evenings to find and synthesize so much data, but the research team was more than up to the task. I owe a special thank you to each of the members of that research group—Matthew St. John, Maureen Hough, Elizabeth Hansen, Paul Ciarcia, Michael Brewer, Brian Caulfield and Chuck Lindberg. Their work with this material helped further shape and advance my own thinking on the topics covered by this book, while their level of professionalism and insight was impressive.

Guiding the work of that team and vital to this project was Andrew Walther, Vice President for Media, Research and Development at the Knights of Columbus. In addition to overseeing our polling over the past two years, his unique combination of insight, energy, and candor—and his feedback on each draft of the manuscript—added significantly to this book, while he simultaneously managed the often difficult task of keeping the production on schedule.

Part of the beauty of books, made more pronounced in the digital age, is the physical design and layout, and in this area Michelle McCleary surpassed herself. She has made each page a physically attractive place for the ideas it contains, and I appreciate all she did, her talent and the hard work it took to achieve this.

Working with Trace Murphy and Doubleday on this project, as on previous books, was a truly great experience. Publishing is Trace's passion, and he brings that and his commitment to excellence to every project. I am very grateful for the assistance, thoughtful advice, critiques, flexibility and accessibility he provided me and this manuscript, as well as his excellent and most valuable support. I am indeed fortunate to have him as my editor.

To all of these individuals—and to the many other people who had some role in the production of this book—my heartfelt thanks.

Foreword

Every book has its purpose, its niche, its raison d'être. This one was written to contribute to the national conversation about what direction the country ought to take based not on a partisan political approach, but on the moral sense—and consensus—of the American people.

The title of this book—*Beyond a House Divided*—is, of course, a reference to the famous warning of our 16th president. Speaking as his party's candidate for the U.S. Senate in Illinois in 1858, Abraham Lincoln cautioned of the implications of the debate on slavery saying, "A house divided against itself cannot stand. I believe this government cannot endure, permanently half slave and half free."

Today, while many see America as a "house divided" over issues of every kind, our surveys have found something very different: unity among the American people based on a moral core of values and ethics. The American people have reached a consensus united—even if some of our institutions have not.

Lincoln's opening words that night in 1858 set the tone for this book. "If we could first know where we are, and whither we are tending, we could then better judge what to do, and how to do it." This is why we have asked the questions we have, in the hope that the answers will help us learn "what to do and how to do it."

Rather than starting at the political poles and moving toward the center on the basis of compromise, this book will argue for a different starting point, for beginning our conversation where the vast majority of the American people stand and seeking first the common ground already found in the common sense of a consensus of the electorate.

This is not an attempt to be the last word on—or the most in depth look at—every contentious issue in the United States today. It is instead intended as a photo album filled with a series of snap shots of the sense—and in many cases the overlooked consensus— of the great majority of the American people. To provide these snap shots, we have looked at recent polling data both our own—conducted by the Marist Institute for Public Opinion since 2008 as part of our Moral Compass Project—and those of other key pollsters including Gallup, Rasmussen, Pew and Zogby. In sifting through a huge volume of polling data, and in asking in our own polling more detailed questions—or focusing on areas not typically treated—we believe we have something meaningful to add to the discussion of American values and to the arguments of the many who have written about our nation as more than just a series of "red" and "blue" states.

In dealing with many high profile issues, we have found consensus where conventional wisdom would have us believe it is most unlikely: on the issues of religion in public life, abortion, marriage, and the role of government, among others. Far from a house divided, Americans are—on issue after issue—united in their common beliefs.

The purpose here is not to suggest that we should have government by polling—using polls crassly for political advantage on one issue or another. Rather, this book uses polling to show that Americans share key values, that our values as Americans are not unlike those on which this country was founded, and that the morality of decisions continues to be very important.

Since this is a book about American values, we have chosen for our definition of consensus one endorsed by the Founders of the country: a two-thirds majority, which is the number needed to over-ride a veto or ratify a treaty. In those areas where the consensus is even greater—three-quarters or more—we feel comfortable declaring a "super consensus"—that is, a sense held in common by an overwhelming majority of the American people.

Particularly in the last two years, as our economy has faltered and we have continued to face an extremely polarized political process, unsurprisingly, many others have taken on some portion of these issues. This includes those who have analyzed the pulse of the American people in various ways, like John Zogby, Frank Luntz and Scott Rasmussen; those who have explored the polarization within Washington and the disconnect it often has from the rest of America like Cal Thomas and Bob Beckel, Ronald Brownstein, Stanley B. Greenberg, Samuel J. Abrams and Jeremy C. Pope; and those who have brought faith and morals to the discussion of economic, political, and social improvement, like the Acton Institute and its *Journal of Markets and Morality*, or Jim Wallis, especially in his most recent book; and many other commentators. Although with each of these this book will have areas of convergence and areas of divergence, I would draw these to the attention of readers interested in additional treatments of the topics.

In particular, this book recognizes that Americans want their voice heard in Washington, and feel that their voice is not heard there or expressed in public policy on certain issues. Beginning with their voice, by looking at the latest and most detailed polling data available, I hope that this book can help propel forward our national conversation—in our homes as well as in Washington, Wall Street, and the Media—about who we are as Americans, what direction we would like to see our country headed, and how we— rather than pundits—think we can get there.

Beyond
a House
Divided

I

Beyond a House Divided: Our Moral Compass

As Americans, we all sense something's wrong. Washington, Wall Street and the media all see it. Our religious leaders, our educators, our commentators all see it. America is unhappy, disillusioned and even angry. What Washington, Wall Street and the media are missing is that the target of the anger is not one party or one politician, it isn't directed at one newspaper or television show, it isn't ire at one hedge fund or another, it's many things. We lack confidence in the trusted institutions that are the foundation of this country.

Every year, new polls about trust come out that show how bad things have gotten. Congress is a perennial favorite, but recently bankers have sunk to new lows, joining the usual suspects such as lawyers and journalists.

What does that say about us as a country when we've lost confidence in the institutions that should be guiding us, and we don't think our country is headed in the right direction?

A generation ago, the fictional character Howard Beale captured a similar mood in the film *Network*, when he faced the public and told them:

> I don't have to tell you things are bad. Everybody knows things are bad. It's a depression. Everybody's out of work or scared of losing their job. The dollar buys a nickel's worth; banks are going bust. . . . There's nobody anywhere who seems to know what to do, and there's no end to it.[1]

Thirty-four years later, Americans—by a two to one margin— think the country is headed in the wrong direction, according to a recent Bloomberg poll.[2] Several other polls show a similar spread.

And there is no need for Americans to be exhorted to follow Beale's advice and "get mad" since 72 percent already agree with his statement, "I'm as mad as hell and I am not going to take it anymore," according to polling in 2008 and 2009 by Frank Luntz.[3]

Figure 1: The Moral Compass

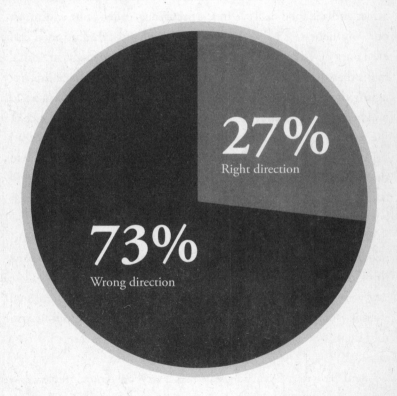

Do you believe the moral compass of this country is pointing in the right direction or the wrong direction?

The Knights of Columbus/Marist Poll July 2010 Survey

But anger isn't the answer, especially for those of us who still believe in the power of America's institutions to be a force for good in the greatest nation in history.

After reading the headlines or hearing the debates in government, we might well conclude that as a nation we face an economic crisis, a financial crisis, a debt crisis, a war crisis, an immigration crisis, a healthcare crisis, a partisanship crisis, a regulatory crisis. But there's another foundational crisis that most Americans believe exists—a moral crisis.

When I began looking at and writing about moral issues in society and the morality of the marketplace in depth, the economic problems that began in 2008 were still a long way off. It was 2006 and 2007, and I was working on my book *A Civilization of Love*, in which I discussed economy from a global and personal business perspective, especially in the chapters about globalization and marketplace ethics. At the time, aside from the Enron scandal of some years before, there were no major market or nationwide wakeup calls to reexamine the economic climate. There were signs—but they were largely ignored. We were still in a stage in which, to borrow the observations of Jim Collins, negative data was prematurely discounted or explained away.[*] We were in the high-point before the fall.

What was a call to better business practices in 2007 sparked the following questions in 2008, especially in light of the market crash: how feasible is more ethical business? And what do Americans think of morality in the marketplace?

Thus in 2008, working with Marist Institute for Public Opinion, the Knights of Columbus began work on our Moral Compass Project, with the goal of testing these views with the views of the American people. What we have found beginning in early 2009 and continuing to the present, was less a conflict of "sides" on issues, and more a consensus on motivations: the motivation which drives Americans day after day, the motivations which should—and should

Table 1: Influence People or Institutions Have on the Moral Direction of the Country

	Right Direction	Wrong Direction	No Effect
Volunteers	73%	5%	22%
Charitable organizations	61%	15%	24%
The U.S. military	55%	24%	21%
Private education	55%	22%	23%
Law enforcement	51%	30%	19%
Families	50%	36%	14%
Doctors	50%	20%	30%
Religious values	48%	35%	17%
Scientists	47%	26%	27%
Religious leaders	43%	38%	19%
Public education	40%	46%	14%
Judges	37%	44%	19%
The Internet	27%	52%	21%
Your state or local government	25%	60%	15%
Federal government	21%	66%	13%
Lawyers	21%	59%	20%
News media	18%	68%	14%
Professional athletes	17%	62%	21%
Business executives	15%	63%	22%
Immigrants	15%	59%	26%
Entertainment industry	13%	73%	14%
Politicians	10%	82%	8%

Do you think each of the following people or institutions are mostly moving the moral compass of this country in the right direction, the wrong direction or have no effect?

The Knights of Columbus/Marist Poll July 2010 Survey

not—guide business decisions, and the motivations of the nation as it faces some of the most difficult days of recent memory.

In our project to track what's important to the American people, we polled on the direction of our country's moral compass. And what we found was that more than two-thirds of Americans believe the *morality* of the country is headed in the wrong direction.[5]

As Americans, we are disillusioned with the institutions that we traditionally look to for guidance in a time like this. Our polling shows that Americans believe each of the following institutions is moving the country in the wrong moral direction.

- Politicians (82%)
- Entertainment Industry (73%)
- News Media (68%)
- Federal Government (66%)
- Business Executives (63%)
- State and Local Governments (60%)
- Lawyers (59%)
- The Internet (52%)

The majorities in most instances include at a minimum Independents and the majority of one or both parties. But perhaps most significantly, in many instances Republicans, Democrats and Independents are in accord.[5]

Many commentators suggest that the country is in the midst of what journalist Ronald Brownstein's book recently called *The Second Civil War*. The effect of that war, the book's subtitle says, is *how extreme partisanship has paralyzed Washington and polarized America.*[6]

But it's not a problem of this segment of the population against that one. It has become a problem of a large consensus of the population at odds with governmental, media and financial institutions.

Many Americans have come to believe these institutions don't see problems the way that we do. Politicians and the media see a world of right and left. The American people see a world of right and wrong.

It's not a quaint idea, it's a foundational one.

President George Washington noted in his farewell address:

> It is substantially true that virtue or morality is a necessary spring of popular government. The rule, indeed, extends with more or less force to every species of free government. Who that is a sincere friend to it can look with indifference upon attempts to shake the foundation of the fabric?[7]

A Harris Poll in February 2010 found that Americans think—with more than 80 percent consensus—that big business, banks and financial institutions, lobbyists and political action committees all have too much power in influencing government policy in Washington. In addition, strong majorities—by more than 30 percentage points—agreed that the news media, entertainment and sports celebrities, and trial lawyers have too much influence.[8]

What institutions do strong majorities of Americans think have "too little" influence in Washington?

By 54 to 35 percent, they say churches and religious groups. By 52 to 32 percent, they say racial minorities. By more than three to one they want non-profit organizations to have more influence, and by more than 20 to one (93 percent to four percent), they think small businesses should.[9]

What is particularly telling is that the American public wants its opinion taken into consideration. By 55 to 31 percent, Americans say opinion polls don't have enough influence, and by more than six to one (82 percent to 13 percent), they say "public opinion" itself should have more influence.[10]

They don't trust the officials who should be listening to public opinion in government, or those reporting on it in the media, but they do trust—overwhelmingly—the sense of the American people, and they want those opinions to be heard and acted upon.

What do they see as moving the moral compass of the country in the right direction?

Overwhelmingly, Americans respond with two answers: charitable organizations (61 percent) and volunteers (73 percent). Pluralities or slight majorities also indicate the U.S. military, families, law enforcement, private education and religious values are moving the country's moral compass in the right direction.[11]

Disappointed by traditional institutions, Americans see altruism as the safe harbor for hope in the future.

And we know what altruism is. According to our survey of Americans by generation, 67 percent have donated money to charity in the last year, and the same percentage indicated that they had volunteered their time in some way.[12] Interestingly, even when simply asked if they had "volunteered for community service" in the past year, one-third said yes.[13] That number doubles when people are given a list of activities and asked if they engage in any of them. It is as though volunteering is so engrained in their lives that they don't even realize it is considered "volunteering." It is—it seems—just what they do.

Religion, too, is a common thread in the tapestry of American life. For Americans, the top two goals are to get married and have a family, and to be spiritual or get closer to God.[14] This is a country, after all, where 84 percent believe in God.[15]

It's also a country founded on religious principles, and whose greatest steps forward—the emancipation of slaves in the 19th century and the civil rights movement a century later—were both couched in religious terms. President Abraham Lincoln, for example, invoked God often during the Civil War—in his second inaugural address and in many letters. At Gettysburg, he made it clear that this nation was distinctly "under God."[16]

The Reverend Martin Luther King, Jr. saw the same. Writing from a Birmingham jail just a couple of months shy of the 100th anniversary of the Battle of Gettysburg, he wrote:

> One day the South will know that when these disinherited children of God sat down at lunch counters, they were in reality standing up for what is best in the American dream and for the most sacred values in our Judaeo Christian heritage, thereby bringing our nation back to those great wells of democracy which were dug deep by the founding fathers in their formulation of the Constitution and the Declaration of Independence.[17]

Holding these values, most Americans agree on a fundamental truth: The country needs a moral compass in its public and private spheres. This should come as no surprise in a country in which our polling found nearly eight in 10 people hold religion to be an important part of their daily life—with well over half saying it's "very" or "extremely" important.[18]

Some, like Boston College professor Alan Wolfe, have argued that:

> ". . . the old adage that America is a free country has, at last, come true, for Americans have come to accept the relevance of individual freedom, not only in their economic and political life, but in their moral life as well."[19]

At first blush, some polling data would seem to support that. Our data showed that a slight majority of all Americans believe that morals are relative: In other words, there is no definite right and wrong.[20] Such a self-opinion, however, belies Americans' true views

Table 2: Life Goals

	Millennials	Gen X	Baby Boom	Greatest
To be spiritual or close to God	31%	17%	19%	21%
To get married and have a family	27%	24%	27%	49%
To get rich	11%	18%	15%	9%
To be an expert in your field	10%	12%	7%	6%
To have fun	8%	12%	11%	4%
To help people who need help	7%	9%	10%	5%
To have close friends	5%	5%	7%	6%
To be a leader in your community	1%	2%	2%	<1%
To be famous	<1%	<1%	1%	1%

Which of the following do you think best captures your top long-term life goal?

The Knights of Columbus/Marist Poll January 2010 Survey

on issue after issue, for when asked specifically for their opinion on various moral issues—even when given the option of "not a moral issue"—a clear moral consensus emerges. On everything from marital infidelity to greed to abortion, Americans are clear—by large majorities—when they find something "morally wrong."[21]

In fact, we found that three-quarters or more of Americans believe marriage, respect for others, and personal responsibility are all undervalued. More than two-thirds say the same of integrity, hard work and work ethic. Almost as many see the law and tolerance of others (both 64 percent), and concern for the less fortunate

(62 percent) this way, and half or more say the same for belief in God (56 percent) and religious observance (54 percent). Americans see all of these as not valued enough in our society.[22]

Most seem united in adhering to the principles that made our nation great, and the moral compass that led to the overcoming of the evils of slavery and segregation. But overcoming those evils took both a moral compass and a capacity for partisans to forgive, to call each other to the "better angels of our nature," as President Lincoln put it in his first inaugural.[23]

Four years later, at his second inaugural, President Lincoln concluded by saying:

> With malice toward none, with charity for all, with firmness in the right as God gives us to see the right, let us strive on to finish the work we are in, to bind up the nation's wounds, to care for him who shall have borne the battle and for his widow and his orphan, to do all which may achieve and cherish a just and lasting peace among ourselves and with all nations.[24]

Americans seem to want to hear this message again.

When one stops classifying people as interest groups and tries to understand how they exist as a community defined by their common values, the social landscape is not necessarily defined by factionalism. In fact, seen through the lens of moral consensus, a different picture emerges that tells us much more about the American character.

On basic moral questions, on what they believe at their core, most Americans stand shoulder to shoulder. They agree that morality has a place not only in our families and personal relationships but also in corporate offices and boardrooms on Wall Street, in the country's newsrooms and in the halls of political power in Washington.

They want to look to family and religion for guidance in their lives. More than 75 percent think that hard work, integrity and education are the keys to personal success.[25]

It's the same with topic after topic. Americans see personal integrity and hard work as the key in their own lives, and want to see strong ethics—at home, in politics and in business. As noted earlier, large majorities—a consensus in fact—think religious values have a proper place, and Americans of all political stripes see a moral crisis in American life. In short, polling—our own and that of other researchers—has found that leaving behind the procrustean bed of left and right, the great moral center of America speaks with far more unanimity than division and wants to make itself heard.

But for some reason, it seems to Americans in general—and to those who follow news, business and politics in particular—that our leaders are not paying attention.

We still live in a representative democracy, but those being represented seem to be the special interests, while the rest of us constitute a quiet consensus. The moral compass at the grassroots level shows us a way forward, but it will require our "institutions"—government, media, entertainment and financial—to have the courage to buck the forces of greed and special interests and to move ahead in a way that can mend the country, rather than simply provide the same old debates as if the mythical divisions between Americans actually exist.

2

Beyond the Wall of Separation: Religion in America

When Americans discuss the role of religion in public life, it is almost inevitable that one will hear reference to the "wall of separation" between church and state—a phrase coined by our third president. Far less often do we recall the words of our first president, who observed that religion and morality are the "indispensable supports" and "firmest props" of good government.

President George Washington's famous farewell address of 1796 was an observation about what early on had set America apart, as well as a roadmap for a fledgling nation already wrestling with its international identity and factional politics. In it, President Washington voiced his concerns over growing sectionalism, stressed the need for a limited government restrained by the Constitution and separate branches of power, and praised the elements of American life that had contributed to the nation's birth.

His speech is most remembered today for his admonition that Americans avoid foreign entanglements. Less remembered is that he particularly praised the role of religious and moral values as important to the creation and future of the United States. "Of all the dispositions and habits which lead to political prosperity, religion and morality are indispensable supports," President Washington said. He continued:

In vain would that man claim the tribute of patriotism, who should labor to subvert these great pillars of human happiness, these firmest props of the duties of men and citizens. The mere politician, equally with the pious man, ought to respect and to cherish them. A volume could not trace all their connections with private and public felicity. Let it simply be asked: Where is the security for property, for reputation, for life, if the sense of religious obligation desert the oaths which are the instruments of investigation in courts of justice? And let us with caution indulge the supposition that morality can be maintained without religion. Whatever may be conceded to the influence of refined education on minds of peculiar structure, reason and experience both forbid us to expect that national morality can prevail in exclusion of religious principle.

It is substantially true that virtue or morality is a necessary spring of popular government. The rule, indeed, extends with more or less force to every species of free government. Who that is a sincere friend to it can look with indifference upon attempts to shake the foundation of the fabric?[1]

When President Washington's address appeared in newspapers throughout the United States, the French writer Alexis de Tocqueville had not yet been born. However, 35 years later, the young author of *Democracy in America* would likewise note the fundamental role that religion and morals served in American life.

On my arrival in the United States, it was the religious aspect of the country that first struck my eye. [. . .] Among us [Europeans], I had seen the spirit of religion and the spirit of freedom almost always move in contrary directions. Here I found them united intimately with one another: they reigned together on the same soil.[2]

Nearly two centuries later, though, the notion of morality and religion—particularly religion—as "indispensable supports" of civic life in the United States seems much more controversial. From lawsuits challenging Nativity scenes on town greens to criticism of religious leaders speaking out on policy matters, President Washington's image of faith-based convictions serving as a pillar in American life has been replaced in the minds of a vocal segment of the population with President Thomas Jefferson's "wall of separation" between church and state. The First Amendment's protection of freedom of religion is now sometimes turned around to justify attempts to completely exclude anything religious from government land, buildings, institutions and the public square in general.

Indeed, on April 13, 2009—the day after Easter—*Newsweek's* cover story carried the ominous headline, "The End of Christian America."

To *Newsweek*'s credit, the article steered clear of a complete eulogy for Christianity in America, but it had this to say about the perceived decline of Christian morality's influence in public life:

> While we remain a nation decisively shaped by religious faith, our politics and our culture are, in the main, less influenced by movements and arguments of an explicitly Christian character than they were even five years ago. I think this is a good thing—good for our political culture, which, as the American Founders saw, is complex and charged enough without attempting to compel or coerce religious belief or observance. It is good for Christianity, too, in that many Christians are rediscovering the virtues of a separation of church and state that protects what Roger Williams, who founded Rhode Island as a haven for religious dissenters, called "the garden of the church" from "the wilderness of the world."[3]

While certainly nuanced, such a statement is not without controversy—both in its interpretation of the Founders' original intent and in its view that faith has increasingly vanished from politics and our national discourse. At its heart, the argument today for the

"wall of separation" in the public square asserts that there is an un-
marked line of demarcation over which Americans of faith must
not cross, lest they upset the secularist balance of society. The
dichotomy it presents is this: Politics is governed either by the im-
position of religious beliefs, or by the near-exclusion of religion.

Such a forced—and false—choice does not fit with the sensibili-
ties of Americans as a whole. The truth is that religion remains
deeply embedded in the American consciousness, and in American
history. The Founding Fathers never intended to create a society that
excludes religious expression from political discourse or public life.
Taken in its proper context, not even Jefferson's famed "wall of separation" tries to do such a thing. Polling shows that a consensus of
Americans don't want to see their country bereft of its longstanding
tradition of protecting religious freedom, or removed from its foundation of religious principles. Rather, they appreciate the contribu-
tion of religious and moral values to the fabric of American life.

Ironically, the week before *Newsweek* proclaimed "The End of
Christian America," we released a survey that showed that almost
two-thirds (63 percent) of Americans and three-quarters (74 percent)
of the nation's largest religious denomination—Catholics—planned
to celebrate Easter by attending church services.[4] *Newsweek's* Easter
article noted that the number of those who say they have no religious
affiliation nearly doubled to 15 percent since 1990.[5]

Religion may not be quite as prominent in America as it once
was. However, that isn't the whole story.

While affiliation with a particular denomination or religion
has declined somewhat, nearly all Americans—an impressive
84 percent—believe in God.[6] Even more telling, more than eight in
10 Americans would vote for a politician who would "stand for the
Christian principles on which this country was founded," with more
than half saying they "definitely would" vote for such a person.[7]

Another trend in Americans' religiosity that pollsters and the
media like to cover is the nation's acceptance of moral relativity. But

a deeper look at the numbers reveals that Americans are not as laissez-faire toward moral issues as they may think they are.

On one hand, our own polling shows that 56 percent of Americans believe "morals are relative; that is, there is no definite right and wrong for everybody."[8] Some issues once considered morally wrong are now more tolerated. For example, 28 percent of Americans believe that having children out of wedlock is acceptable, and divorce and premarital sex are likewise less frowned upon.[9]

However, though 56 percent of Americans may describe morality as relative, when asked whether specific actions are morally wrong, morally acceptable, or not a moral issue, at least a majority of Americans still make a moral judgment on the 16 issues we polled. In fact, on 11 of those issues, a minimum of seven in 10 Americans made a moral judgment.[10]

Our polling also found that nearly three-quarters of Americans consider religion to be important in their lives.[11] Not only do they believe, but they also practice their faith. We found that a third of Americans attend church at least once a week. More than four in 10 (41 percent) go at least once a month, and less than a quarter (24 percent) go once a year or less, or never at all.[12]

The findings from Gallup are comparable. They found that six in 10 Americans are members of a church or synagogue. Nearly a third of Americans attend religious services at least once a week, and 55 percent attend religious services at least once a month.[13]

The numbers may be less than they once were, but compared to other Western countries—particularly those in Europe—our rates of religious attendance and observance are nearly double the norm.

In Europe, in 11 EU countries for which data is available, church attendance is significantly less frequent than in the United States. Only 17 percent attend at least weekly, with monthly attendance at 27 percent.[14]

Yet even if church attendance is down in America, religion certainly is not forgotten. Far from giving up their faith, the vast

Table 1: Moral Choices

	Morally Acceptable	Morally Wrong	Not a Moral Issue
Claiming someone else's work as your own	2%	92%	6%
Marital infidelity	3%	90%	7%
Business decisions motivated by greed	6%	74%	20%
Increasing profits by decreasing the quality of a product or service	4%	70%	26%
Drug use	4%	59%	37%
Abortion	19%	56%	25%
Same-sex marriage	23%	54%	23%
Economic development at the expense of the environment	5%	52%	43%
Gay and lesbian relations	22%	51%	27%
Euthanasia	25%	50%	25%
Having a baby outside of marriage	28%	46%	26%
Medical testing on animals	23%	42%	35%
Sex between an unmarried man and a woman	34%	39%	27%
Medical research using stem cells obtained from human embryos	38%	32%	30%
Divorce	33%	29%	38%
Gambling	26%	25%	49%

Regardless of whether or not you think it should be legal, do you believe that, in general, each one of the following issues is morally acceptable or morally wrong?

The Knights of Columbus/Marist Poll January 2010 Survey

majority of Americans, 64 percent, want to learn more about it.[15] A similar percentage of Americans—63 percent—look to religion for guidance in their lives. Only "family" is more relied upon for direction.[16] And in terms of what values Americans want to pass on to their children, the most popular choice is "faith in God" (33 percent). The next choice, too, had biblical roots: "Treat others as you want to be treated" (27 percent).[17] In other words, 60 percent of Americans look to pass on faith-based values to the next generation. This stands to reason when you consider that 63 percent of Americans pray at least once every day, according to a Rasmussen survey.[18]

The importance of religion in the lives of Americans should not be understated or written off.

Figure 2: Lessons to Teach Children

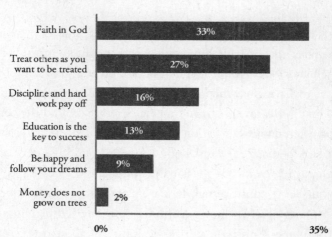

Which one of the following do you believe is the most important value or lesson to teach your children?

The Knights of Columbus/Marist Poll July 2010 Survey

In fact, on many core religious values, we found that Americans have achieved consensus. From upholding marital fidelity to considering religious values a beneficial guide in the workplace, Americans—on issue after issue—continue to see things through a values lens our grandparents would recognize.

As mentioned earlier, the vast majority of us would vote for a candidate who stands for the nation's founding Christian principles. More than half "definitely would." Even more Americans—93 percent—would vote for a politician who would "uphold religious liberty and freedom of conscience," and nearly two-thirds (65 percent) "definitely would."[19]

Religion has long informed a large percentage of the American electorate, and far from being consigned to the margins of our lives, it continues to influence us today.

Religious values were core principles in the founding of the United States.

But even more hotly debated than Americans' level of religious identity is the level of intersection that ought to exist between church and state. From the mention of God at a high school graduation to Christmas-themed ornaments in civic spaces, such battles—in courts, town halls and media coverage around the country—too often depict our nation as "a house divided" by religion.

In fact, perhaps the most hotly contested public display of religion in America in 2010 was barely public and went for decades without being controversial. It was a single cross in the middle of the Mojave Desert, which—as Justice Anthony Kennedy noted in the Supreme Court's majority decision to allow the cross to remain—was erected more in honor of fallen veterans than as a symbol proclaiming the tenets of Christianity.[20] Nevertheless—remote desert location or not—a vocal minority continue to argue that symbols like these have no place in the public square, or in this case, on public land. They believe that religion poses a danger to our system of government and that the "wall of separation" should thus divide religious values and expression from the state.

Certainly those who support this view have been successful in getting noticed, but despite the rhetoric and reporting that can make it seem like the country is evenly divided over the issue of religion in public life, we are far from a 50/50 split.

Most Americans believe religion ought to have a place in the public square. Far from feeling afflicted or threatened by expressions of faith in public life, 76 percent of Americans favor the display of religious symbols on public land, according to Rasmussen.[21]

More often than not, the final say in the matter belongs to the courts, a fact that is a point of controversy in itself. According to surveys from Rasmussen, nearly half of Americans (46 percent) believe the U.S. Supreme Court is too hostile toward religion, while only 13 percent characterize the Court as "too friendly."[22] By a three to one margin (64 percent to 21 percent), almost two-thirds of Americans believe judges' rulings have been more anti-religious than the Founding Fathers intended.[23] In the wake of a federal court decision in April 2010 that found the country's National Day of Prayer unconstitutional, a Rasmussen poll showed six in 10 Americans favor the federal government recognizing a National Day of Prayer.[24] Rasmussen also found that the majority of Americans also favor the incorporation of more religious observance into public education. Six in 10 Americans support allowing students to pray in public schools,[25] and a super-consensus—more than eight in 10—supports the celebration of at least some religious holidays in public schools.[26] Similarly, 82 percent of Americans oppose the removal of the words "under God" from the Pledge of Allegiance, and 77 percent of Americans believe that school children should recite the Pledge every morning.[27]

Figure 3: Religious Expression

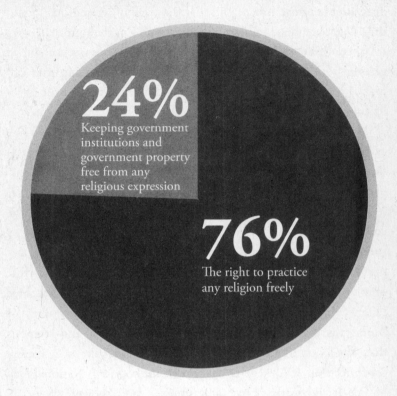

24%
Keeping government
institutions and
government property
free from any
religious expression

76%
The right to practice
any religion freely

Which is more important to you?

The Knights of Columbus/Marist Poll July 2010 Survey

But this isn't just an issue of religious symbols in courthouses or the politics of prayer in school. As we have discussed, Americans believe in God, and most of us pray, want to learn more about our faith, want religious ethics at work and at home, and look to religion for guidance in our daily lives.

Rather than wishing to exclude religious observance from public life, Americans—in numbers that can only be described as a consensus—embrace the benefits that religious values and institutions offer society.

Our polling showed Americans, by more than a three to one margin (76 percent to 24 percent), are more interested in protecting the freedom to practice one's religion than in stripping government land and institutions of all references to religion.[28] That consensus—and its consistency with the history of the country—should be the starting point for discussions on this issue.

The American people today are quite in line with the Founders' vision for the role of religion in the United States.

Those who fight to create what the late Reverend Richard John Neuhaus described as the "naked public square"—even if that square is the far-reaches of the Mojave Desert—should perhaps reassess the secular orthodoxy that seeks to push into private any religious symbols or principles, even nonsectarian ones.

The phrase "wall of separation" comes from a letter by President Thomas Jefferson, the nation's third president, to the Danbury Baptist Association in Connecticut. Since he penned it some 200 years ago, it has arguably become a convenient catch phrase in this debate for those seeking a fully secular country. But it is the interpretation of the meaning and implication of President Jefferson's words that has created the controversy more than the meaning of the letter—or President Jefferson's thinking—itself.

In his dissenting opinion to *Wallace v. Jaffree* (1985), Supreme Court Justice William Rehnquist expressed further criticism of the jurisprudence founded on Jefferson's letter to the Danbury Baptist Association, noting that the Constitution's Establishment Clause "has been expressly freighted with Jefferson's misleading metaphor for nearly 40 years."

Justice Rehnquist likewise observed that the concept of the wall of separation had actually made the Court's First Amendment jurisprudence inconsistent, writing:

Notwithstanding the absence of a historical basis for this theory of rigid separation, the wall idea might well have served as a useful, albeit misguided analytical concept, had it led this Court to unified and principled results in Establishment Clause cases. The opposite, unfortunately, has been true. [. . .]

[O]ur Establishment Clause cases have been neither principled nor unified. Our recent opinions, many of them hopelessly divided pluralities, have with embarrassing candor conceded that the "wall of separation" is merely a "blurred, indistinct, and variable barrier" which "is not wholly accurate" and can only be "dimly perceived."

He concluded, "The 'wall of separation between church and State' is a metaphor based on bad history, a metaphor which has proved useless as a guide to judging. It should be frankly and explicitly abandoned."[29]

President Jefferson's letter is poor evidence when considering the intent of the Framers of the Constitution. Not only was Thomas Jefferson in France when the Bill of Rights was passed by Congress, but the letter to the Danbury Baptist Association was, as Justice Rehnquist described, "a short note of courtesy, written 14 years after the Amendments were passed by Congress," and it was probably not intended by the president to be the basis for future jurisprudence.[30]

In his original draft, President Jefferson crossed out the words "be assured that your religious rights shall never be infringed by any act of mine,"[31] giving us a sense of what he was thinking. This was not a president afraid of Baptists taking over the government, but a president writing to reassure Baptists that his government would not interfere with their practice of their religion. President Jefferson did not want any established religion infringing on the rights of any other, and at the time, Baptists feared the Constitution of the State of Connecticut, which maintained the Congregational Church as an established religion and continued to do so until 1818.

President Jefferson may have frowned on an established sectarian religion, but he didn't shy away from the use of general religious imagery. This was a president who at his second inauguration in 1805—three years after the letter to the Danbury Baptist Association—told the nation that he would need "the favor" of the, "Being in whose hands we are, who led our forefathers, as Israel of old," to "enlighten the minds of your [public] servants, guide their councils, and prosper their measures, that whatsoever they do, shall result in your good, and shall secure to you the peace, friendship, and approbation of all nations."[32]

If he were a man who truly wanted to keep a wall between *all* things religious and civic, he would have been hard-pressed to deliver such a speech to the nation.

Neither at the beginning of our national history nor in the minds of the vast majority of the public today has the intention of the First Amendment been understood to exclude religion from the public square. Instead, a consensus understands it as a way to ensure Americans have the right to practice whatever religion they choose. So long as the government does not interfere with freedom of religion or force a sectarian belief on the people, Americans believe that religion can continue to be an "indispensable support" to the edifice of our democratic institutions.

As Alexis de Tocqueville wrote:

Religion, which, among Americans, never mixes directly in the government of society, should therefore be considered as the first of their political institutions; for if it does not give them the taste for freedom, it singularly facilitates their use of it. [. . .] They believe it necessary to the maintenance of republican institutions . . .[33]

No credible voices today seek to impose sectarian religious rule on this country. The bigger issue we confront is a society in which a small number of people have tried to paint any religious expression as the "establishment of religion"—even if the expression is non-sectarian or as harmless as an ornamental angel on a Christmas tree.

In fact, though discussed less often than the First Amendment, the Constitution does have something to say about bringing one's conscience and religious beliefs into the public square. Article VI states: "No religious Test shall ever be required as a Qualification to any Office or public Trust under the United States."[34] As then-presidential candidate John F. Kennedy eloquently put it when his Catholic faith became an issue in the 1960 election:

> [I]f this election is decided on the basis that 40 million Americans lost their chance of being president on the day they were baptized, then it is the whole nation that will be the loser—in the eyes of Catholics and non-Catholics around the world, in the eyes of history, and in the eyes of our own people.[35]

At his inauguration, President Kennedy's belief in God did not strike a sectarian note. Instead, it was based on the common belief in God he shared with the Founders, a belief that aligned him with the "same revolutionary beliefs for which our forebears fought"—namely, "the belief that the rights of man come not from the generosity of the state, but from the hand of God."[36]

The Framers of the Constitution would not have advocated for the total exclusion of religion from public life. Indeed they did not, for they saw religious institutions as vital to our democratic experiment. An examination of the historical context provides insight to their intentions: Unlike the monarchies of Europe, which had established churches sponsored by the state, the government of the United States would have no established religion and would extend legal protection to all religious sects and denominations. Though non-sectarian, this system would be founded on the basis that our rights came from God—not the state—and it would hold Judeo-Christian values as the very pillars of its governance.

Today, Americans still recognize the need for religion and religious beliefs in the public square. From business decisions to personal ones, Americans look to family and religion first, and in impressive numbers, and they think it's a good idea for others to do the same.

The American consensus on religion's role in the public discourse is not just a national mood, it's a fact founded in American history. Those few who insist on removing every last reference to religion in every courthouse, in every classroom, on every town green, and in every corner of every desert are out of step with the history of our nation, and with the consensus of its people.

Theocracy is not a danger in 21st-century America. A country in which religion is marginalized is a far more likely outcome.

But Americans want neither, and that profound consensus—so in keeping with our nation's history—should not go unnoticed.

With the overwhelming majority of Americans believing in God and most wanting to learn more about their religion, it's unlikely that this trend will change.

As a people, we want freedom of religion and freedom of conscience. We don't want some sectarian theocracy, nor do we want to topple those "indispensable supports" that religion provides. In short, we want what the Founders gave us, what President Kennedy reaffirmed and what President Lincoln called at Gettysburg a "nation under God."

To deny all religious expression in public places is fundamentally at odds with the idea that our rights come from our creator, not our government. Moving away from that ideal and putting our faith in government—rather than in the unchanging hands of our Creator—is disquieting for the majority of the American people.

3

Beyond Greed: Toward Morality in the Marketplace

"Extraordinary evil," were the words used by the judge to describe the actions of 71-year-old investor Bernard Madoff as he was sentenced to 150 years in prison in the summer of 2009.[1] Madoff's conviction for fraud and money laundering marked the climax in the largest and most elaborate "Ponzi scheme" in American history.[2] He had shattered the life savings and portfolios of many individuals and charitable groups alike. The scheme that resulted in the loss of billions of dollars quickly became the most egregious example of reckless greed in the history of Wall Street and shook people's confidence in an already faltering financial sector.

The Madoff scandal unraveled before an American public already shell-shocked from an economic upheaval that began in the subprime housing market and spread to every sector of the economy. Most—including policymakers, pundits, regulators, executives and investors—had failed to anticipate the fatal flaws in the housing market and now seemed unable to rescue the system. In just one year, between the end of 2007 and the end of 2008, an estimated $6 trillion in wealth was lost.[3]

What happened? Sure, Madoff broke the law, and billions disappeared and a substantial number (more than 40 percent of Americans and American executives) think that crimes like Madoff's are a widespread practice.

But something else occurred under the legal radar. The financial crisis depleted trillions, yet in most cases, those responsible for the unprecedented losses broke no laws and did no jail time—even though the consequences for Americans, who lost vast amounts of their retirements, pensions and savings, were all too real, and the global repercussions of the housing market debacle made the scope of Madoff's crimes pale in comparison.

While many blamed insufficiencies in the laws, regulations and political oversight of Wall Street, others began asking what had happened to right and wrong. How was it that so many people had made so many decisions that left so many destitute—and all within the confines of the law? Was the fault simply one of inappropriate regulation, or was something more fundamental at work: moral bankruptcy on the part of financial managers, institutions and investors?

The crash heightened a crisis of confidence in political and economic institutions that persists to this day.[4] While some—like Madoff—had flouted the law and morality, many more had kept within the law but lost their moral center, and Americans began to wonder whether the country itself had lost its moral bearings.

Moral bearings, of course, could be lost in many ways. Interestingly, in a 2008-2009 poll, Frank Luntz asked Americans, in terms of the traditional "seven deadly sins," which were the worst vices affecting the nation. Looking at our culture, Americans could have argued for any of them. But interestingly, none came close to the first choice—greed. Luntz found that nearly two-thirds of Americans think greed (at 64 percent) is the worst vice affecting Americans as a whole. The other six "deadly sins" polled in the single digits.[5] In other words, not only did greed influence the economy and contribute to the collapse, but most Americans see greed as the preeminent vice in our culture.

And when we asked people specifically about the economic downturn, it was nearly unanimous: Americans, more than 92 percent, believe greed was a major factor in causing the economic crisis. Almost three quarters (71 percent) take the strongest position possible, saying greed had "a great deal" to do with causing the crisis.[6]

The greed was widespread. From banks that aggressively promoted sub-prime mortgages, to real estate speculators, to Wall Street with its appetite for highly structured and speculative transactions—everyone was tempted in the quest for a quick dollar. But the plan was utopian at best, making sense only as long as real estate prices kept increasing and interest rates did not.

With the demise of banks and investment firms went the untold stories of those most hurt by such events. The savings of everyday people were wiped out as greed turned to panic and the market plummeted. The modest homeowner was evicted because of a loan he never could have afforded. Indeed, Gordon Gekko, the fictional character in the film *Wall Street*, who symbolized the Wall Street culture of the 1980s with his proclamation that "greed, for lack of a better word, is good,"[7] found himself without many allies. His mantra was now understood to be as bankrupt as his morals had always been.

Greed found itself opposed by almost everyone: candidates Barack Obama[8] and John McCain,[9] the Acton Institute[10] and Center for American Progress.[11] Whatever their solutions and disagreements, regardless of what they thought was the source of the greed, they all agreed that greed was part of the problem.

Some proposed that greed was a problem that went beyond a legal fix. Yet on both sides of the political aisle, regulation and legislation—not morality—were the primary topics of discussion in terms of finding a solution. For the most part, the only disagreement was over what kind of, and how much, regulation was needed.

"All of us want to deliver a reform that will tighten the screws on Wall Street, but we're not going to be rushed on another massive bill," said Senate Minority Leader Mitch McConnell in April.[12]

Majority leader Harry Reid said of the regulations: "Wall Street reform is preventive care."[13]

What was often missing from public debate in the United States was something that most Americans understood at their moral core: The crisis could not be fixed simply through more legislation or less regulation. Americans sensed that there was an even bigger issue at work that went beyond a legal fix—a forsaking of ethics and moral values, and specifically, a dismissive attitude toward the destructive effects of greed. Certainly laws may be made better, but without an understanding of the crisis as a moral one, without a call for each of us to respond to the "better angels" of our nature, a solution is elusive. The crisis, in essence, was caused by human beings making choices at odds with concern for their neighbor.

A purely legal solution to a moral problem may make good politics or good television, but it does not make good people—on Wall Street or anywhere else. The greedy can always find another loophole, making legal fixes seem like a constant, reactive game of catch-up. After the Enron and WorldCom scandals a decade ago, the Sarbanes-Oxley Act provided a regulatory "fix" to the crisis at hand, but it didn't prevent the meltdown of 2008.

But there were few public calls for a return to a moral sense. So as Congress debated its various regulatory solutions to the economic crisis, we asked Americans what they thought government should do.

Despite Washington's best intentions, people seem skeptical of a legislative fix to the current crisis. We found that a solid majority (55 percent) believe more government regulation "will hurt business and the economy."[14]

Additionally, when it came to cultivating ethics in business, personal responsibility outpolled government responsibility. Fewer than half think the government should play "a major role . . . in making sure Corporate America upholds high ethical standards." By contrast, 79 percent say top executives should play a major role, 69 percent say a company's employees should and 63 percent see a

Table 1: Responsible for Corporate
America's Ethical Standards

Percentage Reporting "Major Role"	
A company's top executives	79%
A company's employees	69%
Shareholders and individual investors	63%
Investment managers	53%
Government	49%
College and University business schools	45%
Religious leaders	30%

*Should each of the following have a major role,
a minor role or no role at all in making sure
Corporate America upholds high ethical standards?*

The Knights of Columbus/Marist Poll July 2010 Survey

major role for "shareholders and individual investors."[15]

At the same time, 70 percent of Americans have little confidence in the government's ability to deal with the financial crisis, according to our poll from July 2010 (47 percent are less confident than a year ago, while 23 percent "remain not confident").[16]

Interestingly, compared to our polling six months earlier, the proportion of Americans who have grown more confident decreased by almost half, from 20 percent in January to 12 percent in July. The total of those showing any confidence at all decreased by 11 percentage points, from 41 percent in January to 30 percent in July.[17]

Perhaps it shouldn't be surprising that Americans don't expect lawmakers to be able to handle the crisis. After all, although our polling shows that exactly half of Americans see the "overall ethical conduct" of corporate executives as poor, politicians are viewed negatively by even more. (More than six in 10 Americans rate their ethical conduct as poor while only eight percent say excellent or good).[18]

In other words, Americans have even less faith in Washington's moral compass than in Wall Street's, which may explain why they're doubtful a regulatory fix can fully repair what has been left shattered in the aftermath of the economic crisis.

There is a real disconnect. In July 2010, Politico found that more than 60 percent of the general population thinks the country is headed in the wrong direction. Tellingly, less than half of Washington insiders share this view; likewise, by a more than three to one ratio, they also admitted that the economic crisis had affected them less than most Americans.[19]

Figure 2: Confidence in Government's Ability to Deal with Economic Crisis

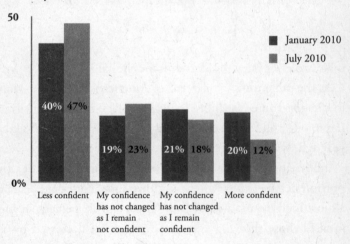

Thinking about the past 12 months, are you more confident or less confident in government's ability to deal with the economic crisis than you were a year ago?

The Knights of Columbus/Marist Poll January and July 2010 Surveys

Table 2: Ethical Conduct of Professions

Percentage Reporting "Poor"	
Politicians	**62%**
Wall Street executives	**57%**
Corporate executives	**50%**
Lawyers	**32%**
Accountants	**10%**
Doctors	**5%**

Would you rate the overall level of honesty and ethical conduct of each of the following professions as excellent, good, fair or poor?

The Knights of Columbus/Marist Poll July 2010 Survey

How Washington reacted to warnings years ago about the impending crisis is also a penetrating glimpse into a culture at times either broken or overly political. Take the Security and Exchange Commission's turning a deaf ear to Harry Markopolos, who for years tried to alert them to Bernie Madoff's scheme.[20] The system that should have worked didn't.

Then there is Armando Falcon, the former head of the Office of Federal Housing Enterprise Oversight. Years before the economic crisis, he warned of problems with the use of derivatives at Fannie Mae and Freddie Mac. In the April 2010 hearing of the FCIC (Financial Crisis Inquiry Commission) regarding Fannie Mae and Freddie Mac, he described a failure of leadership that was "deeply rooted in a culture of arrogance and greed"—a systemic breakdown that made the companies "not unwitting victims of an economic down cycle or flawed products and services of theirs."

In 2004, though, he found his concerns viewed through partisan lenses at a hearing by the Committee on Financial Services.

Symptomatic of what the American people think is wrong with
Washington, they simply wrote him off as "politically motivated"
and dismissed his warnings. Members of both parties came together to urge his ouster in a spending bill in late 2004.[21] The belief that political motivations were behind his report seemed
altogether more important than the report itself.[22]

Just before Christmas, 2004, he described Congressional reaction
in an interview with *The New York Times*:

> Unfortunately, this all got caught up in a political tug of war going on at
> Capitol Hill. [. . .] It became, 'Are you prohousing or antihousing?'
> when what we were trying to do was just address safety and soundness.[23]

Viewed through an overly political lens, the gravity of his report
was distorted. Politics trumped facts and common sense.

In July 2010, Reuters reported that Fannie Mae and Freddie Mac
had received from the U.S. Treasury a total of $145 billion in tax-
payer funds, "a figure that is expected to continue to mount."[24]

Americans have every right to look back on such episodes with
frustration—but the bigger issue is how we move on from here. It's
worth asking: Is greed avoidable? Many of the most respected
voices of the last century have assumed that it is not.

In 1979, Phil Donahue asked Milton Friedman about the benefits of "greed" and self-interest. "But it seems to reward not virtue as
much as ability to manipulate the system," Donahue said. Friedman replied:

> And what *does* reward virtue? You think the communist commissary
> rewards virtue? You think a Hitler rewards virtue? You think (excuse
> me, if you'll pardon me) *American Presidents* reward virtue? Do they
> choose their appointees on the basis of the virtue of the people ap-
> pointed or on the basis of their political clout? Is it really true that po-
> litical self interest is nobler somehow than economic self interest?[25]

Friedman, a Nobel laureate in economics, spent a lifetime defending the value of the freedom of our economic system compared to the straightjacket of communism. History has certainly proved which system was better. But better isn't perfect, and Americans today want to hear a call for morality more than a defense of self-interest even if they agree that politics is no more virtuous than business. In fact, they want to hear the call to morality for both business leaders and politicians.

In an op-ed on the "greed" associated with the rising price of gasoline in 2006, Prof. Gary Galles of Pepperdine University quoted Friedman as saying: "What kind of society isn't structured on greed? The problem of social organization is how to set up an arrangement under which greed will do the least harm." Friedman didn't think greed was good; he wanted to channel it and minimize its destructive potential. If he made a mistake, it is that Friedman may well have agreed with Galles' conclusion that "we cannot change the extent of people's greed."[26]

The power of greed needs no explanation. Any mother who has tried to get her 4-year-old to share a toy with another child knows just how powerful a force it can be. Economists who don't believe "greed is good" do at least often believe that "greed is inevitable."

When I was at the World Economic Forum in Davos, Switzerland, in January 2010, I had the opportunity to listen to Muhammad Yunus, another Nobel laureate, speak on a panel about ethical decision making. Yunus noted that since people can also be altruistic, we should present them with a choice: to be greedy or to be altruistic, becoming social entrepreneurs or having not-for-profit businesses and associations that set as their aim the common good.[27]

Yunus' testimony proved rather provocative—made stronger by his personal experience in bringing a social conscience to the business world through his micro-credit program in Bangledesh—gaining many supporters including Jim Wallis.

Yunus and others have done much good in challenging others to behave altruistically. But perhaps we needn't concede quite so much. Human nature is capable of both greed and altruism. But we need not acquiesce to the inevitability of greed. The fundamental challenge for those in business today is not to set up parallel business worlds, for those motivated by greed and those motivated by a social conscience. In fact, the fundamental challenge is much older than this crisis or any other. The real challenge comes from the question in the first chapters of Genesis: "Am I my brother's keeper?"[28]

How we answer that is telling. Answering, "Yes, I am my brother's keeper" implies two things: First, you claim another person as your brother, and second, you have a responsibility toward him. This responsibility extends beyond family. Corporate America and all of us have responsibilities toward those we interact with— our customers, those we do business with, our shareholders and our employees.

This sort of thinking changes everything—in government, in business, in our social responsibility to others. It means we must consider the broader consequences of our actions.

In Genesis, Cain in effect answers "no" to the question, "Am I my brother's keeper?" after killing his brother out of greed and envy.

That's not to say that greedy people are murderers. But when their greed makes money disappear and a pension plan go belly up—when a widow's life-savings vanish or a family's college tuition nest egg gets scrambled—it's not murder, but it certainly ruins lives.

We are a society in which two-thirds of us think that concern for the less fortunate "is not valued enough," and more than two-thirds say they have donated time and money in the past year.[29] We have a good starting point for "our brother's keeper" thinking. There is almost no support for the sort of personal greed that can leave our brothers and sisters stranded and in need.

Such an alternative economic theory was presented in the 1980s. Like Friedman's, it had no use for the command-and-control communist system. It saw the "determinate" nature of communism—an imposed system of collective will for individual will that renders individual morality irrelevant—as both dangerous and unsustainable. But it warned that some capitalists were making the same mistake if they saw market forces as making morality irrelevant. It had a warning for capitalism: Moral bankruptcy could cause "the laws of the market to collapse."

The man who proposed this wasn't an economist, but a theologian named Joseph Ratzinger—better known to us now as Pope Benedict XVI—writing in a 1985 paper titled "Market, Economy and Ethics."[30]

As we look to repair our economy, we would do well to heed his observation: Capitalism misleads itself when it assumes only self-interest—and not attention to the common good—can successfully guide the market.

It is important to remember that there was a time when "virtue ethics" informed the way business was done. Some have even argued that Adam Smith, whose book *Theory of Moral Sentiments* deals with the subject of virtue at some length, has been inappropriately labeled as an advocate for purely self-interested action.[31] Smith did point out that virtue is not only good but also good for business.

These words from Smith's *Theory of Moral Sentiments* still ring true today:

> By the wise contrivance of the Author of nature, virtue is upon all ordinary occasions, even with regard to this life, real wisdom, and the surest and readiest means of obtaining both safety and advantage.

Smith went on to explain that having a virtuous reputation is a great advantage in business, adding:

Since the practice of virtue, therefore, is in general so advantageous, and that of vice so contrary to our interest, the consideration of those opposite tendencies undoubtedly stamps an additional beauty and propriety upon the one and a new deformity and impropriety upon the other.[32]

No one wants a sleight of hand on Wall Street or a heavy hand from Washington. Americans want "virtue" and a system that allows for sustainable economic development, a system where profit doesn't come at the expense of the common good. In short, they want capitalism with a conscience.

By overwhelming majorities, Americans believe business decisions should be guided by moral choices. We found that three-quarters of Americans believe business leaders should apply the same ethical standards at work as they do in their personal lives, though 81 percent don't believe that usually happens.[33] Nearly two-thirds of Americans (65 percent) think religious values have a place in influencing the ethical decisions of executives;[34] an even greater number of executives, 70 percent, agree.[35] Finally, neither the general population nor executives believe such ethical standards will hurt business: Nearly eight in 10 Americans (79 percent) believe a business can be ethical and successful,[36] and nearly all business executives, 94 percent, agree.[37] In short: Americans rightly understand that ethics don't have to come at the expense of profitability. The failures are clear. So are the solutions. What is needed now is action.

The choice needn't be either capitalism or altruism. One can have a successful market economy with an ethical foundation. Applied to business, the question "am I my brother's keeper?" offers the possibility of success infused with a spirit of responsibility, of service, and of dedication to the common good. It challenges us to be creative and committed to pursuing excellence in business by holding as our guide our high ethical standards.

Such standards can be good for everyone and good for business. The Knights of Columbus is an example of this, not only evidenced in our charitable giving, but also in our success in running a business enterprise based on Catholic social teaching.

We consciously strive to treat both customers and employees fairly, and our investment criteria include a moral component that steers us away from investing in companies whose business operations are at odds with Catholic teaching. These criteria have not reduced our profitability; in fact, over the past decade, our investment returns have been comparable to those of major indices and have remained competitive even in the face of market declines.

In the current economic crisis, the position of the Knights of Columbus has actually improved relative to the rest of the insurance industry. As a result, we've received the highest ratings from A.M. Best and Standard & Poor's, as well as ethical certification from the Insurance Marketplace Standards Association. The Knights of Columbus is one of only two insurance companies in the United States that can lay claim to all three high marks—and the only one in Canada.

In short, we believe that where we invest our money and what companies we choose to partner with are ways we can help influence the moral compass of various businesses for the better. This isn't just something for "another company" to do. Recently, the Associated Press reported on the sustained growth of mutual funds for socially responsible investors (SRI).[38] Such funds' investments often avoid the alcohol, tobacco and weapons industry; other criteria could include a company's environmental practices, its record on community relations, or its outspokenness on human rights. The AP reported that since the 1990s, the number of SRI funds has doubled to around 200. Even when nearly $96 billion disappeared from stock mutual funds during the 2008 crash, SRI funds beat the trend, pulling in $700 million. In terms of performance, the article continued, an index of companies that screen for environmental and social issues showed returns comparable to the S&P 500 at the three- and five-year marks.

In his books on corporate longevity and business success, *Built to Last* and *Good to Great*, author Jim Collins points out that the most successful businesses are those that place "core values" above the exclusive search for monetary profit.[39]

Comparing "visionary" companies to "comparison" companies—similar in many ways, but not in vision—Collins makes a compelling case for the importance of placing values over profit.

Collins uses Ford as one of several examples. He quotes former Ford CEO Don Peterson as saying, "Putting profits after people and products was magical at Ford." Peterson wasn't the first to think that way. As Collins points out, Henry Ford reduced prices in the face of increased demand, paid nearly twice the typical daily wage to his workers, and for his work elicited the following reaction, as Robert Lacy's description—quoted by Collins—makes clear:

> The *Wall Street Journal* accused Henry Ford of "economic blunders if not crimes" which would soon "return to plague him and the industry he represents as well as organized society." In a naïve wish for social improvement, declared the newspaper, Ford had injected "spiritual principles into a field where they do not belong"—a heinous crime—and captains of industry lined up to condemn "the most foolish thing ever attempted in the industrial world."[40]

Following the crash of 2008, as *The New York Times* noted, "A slimmed-down General Motors emerged from bankruptcy as a shadow of the manufacturing titan it had been," the bulk of its assets now government-owned. As for Chrysler, it was "forced into the arms of Fiat." But Ford's story was different:

Ford never asked for cash assistance from the government. Before the recession began, it had set aside $25 billion for a turnaround fund, even borrowing against the company's iconic blue nameplate. That money helped it weather the plunge in sales that affected all car companies when the economy went into sharp decline in the fall of 2008. It did lobby for assistance to its competitors, arguing that a collapse of either GM or Chrysler could put its suppliers out of business and create a domino effect. It was the first of the three to bounce back; the third quarter of 2009 was its first profitable one for its North American operations since 2006.[41]

Figure 3: Factors in Making Business Decisions*

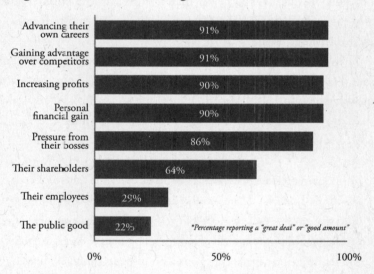

When making business decisions, do you think corporate executives take each of the following factors into account: a great deal, a good amount, not very much or not at all?

The Knights of Columbus/Marist Poll July 2010 Survey

Despite stories such as Ford's, and the overwhelming sense among Americans—and executives—that a business can be ethical and successful, Americans don't think such action is the norm. In a super-consensus, at least 90 percent believe executives' business decisions are based on "advancing their own careers," "gaining advantage over competitors," "increasing profits" or "personal financial gain." Less than a third think executives' decisions take into account "their employees," and less than one-quarter (22 percent) believe "the public good" is a motivating factor.[42]

In a similar survey, more than 90 percent of executives agreed that career, profit, competitive advantage and financial gain top the decision-making matrix. Fewer than a third say "the public good," and just over half say "their employees" are important factors in their decision making.[43]

This "me first" attitude wasn't just the hallmark of those who followed Gordon Gekko's philosophy on Wall Street. At an FCIC inquiry, Armando Falcon described the "profit at all costs" mentality that drove the business dealings even at institutions like Fannie Mae and Freddie Mac. He stated:

> In my opinion, the goals were not the cause of the enterprises' demise. The firms would not engage in any activity, goal fulfilling or otherwise, unless there was a profit to be made. Fannie and Freddie invested in subprime and Alt A mortgages in order to increase profits and regain market share. Any impact on meeting affordable housing goals was a byproduct of the activity.[44]

It's a far cry from Collins's "core values."

Shortly after the fall of European communism two decades ago, then-Czech President Vaclav Havel addressed his nation on the importance of individual responsibility within an economic system. Speaking of the failure of communism, he said:

We live in a morally contaminated environment. We fell morally ill because we became used to saying something different from what we thought. We learned not to believe in anything, to ignore each other, to care only about ourselves. [. . .] We have to understand this legacy as a sin we committed against ourselves. [. . .] If we realize this, hope will return to our hearts.[45]

When he spoke in 1990, the world had just watched transfixed as the Iron Curtain collapsed in Europe. Indeed, one of the two financial and political systems that had defined most of the 20th century almost instantaneously disappeared from the European continent. The idea of atheistic communism as a viable economic force had been debunked, leading at least one commentator to proclaim that "the end of history" was at hand.[46]

But triumphalism can be dangerous, and today with the world economy in the midst of a deep recession, we would do well to keep Havel's words of individual moral responsibility in mind as a necessary part of any real solution.

Most Americans, looking back at the crisis as one of greed and immoral action, can probably agree with Havel—along with many in business—that leaders "learned not to believe in anything, to ignore each other, to care only about [them]selves." Communism failed because it took individual morality out of the equation. We all need to make sure we don't make that same mistake in our market-based system.

The trouble on Wall Street didn't happen in a vacuum. It happened in a country where our institutions became divorced from our values, despite the fact that the data indicate that both executives and the American people know such behavior isn't necessary for success. What remains to be seen is whether America's repudiation of greed and the desire for a return to virtue in the marketplace is genuinely embraced.

Americans have examined their consciences. They know what their values are. Ninety-six percent say if they saw a coworker doing something unethical they would take action—44 percent would report it, and 52 percent would talk to the person directly about his or her ethical lapse.[47]

Americans care about the public good, but Americans and business executives alike agree that all too often business decisions aren't made that way. There is an enormous disconnect between Americans' values and the wavering standards of ethics they see in their business leaders, and Americans expect better. We no longer want to hear that this set of ethics went to market, and that set of ethics stayed home.

We want one set of ethics—not a split-conscience of "business ethics" and "personal ethics." Just ethics will do. Beyond self-interest and partisan ideology, it's time to focus on how to build on Americans' ethical consensus, for the sake of restoring and rescuing our business, political and economic systems—and thus our international standing, our capacity for charity, our parents' retirement and our children's future.

It's time for all of us to listen—to the consensus, to our customers, to our constituents, to the better angels of our nature. This is what the American people are calling for, and it's also the only sustainable way out of the current crisis, and the only way to avoid another one.

4

Beyond Partisan Politics: Values-based Leadership

The American people today have serious concerns about the way government operates. They see gridlock, partisan bickering, a lack of leadership and unceasing, bitter debates.

In July 2010, a Rasmussen poll found that nearly two-thirds of Americans (66 percent) believe politics in Washington will only become more partisan over the next year; only 13 percent foresee a more cooperative future.[1]

Earlier that year, 82 percent of Americans told a Fox News/Opinion Dynamics poll that they are "fed up with and tired of" partisan fighting in the nation's capital, more so than with any other topic raised by the survey.[2]

Ironically, politicians on both sides of the aisle have acknowledged the partisanship crisis. In his book *The Second Civil War: How Extreme Partisanship Has Paralyzed Washington and Polarized America*, journalist Ronald Brownstein quotes Republican Senator Lindsey Graham, who lamented, "You are one team versus the other and never shall the twain meet. If it's a Democratic idea, I have to be against it because it came from a Democrat. And vice versa."[3]

Former Democratic Representative Richard Gephardt expressed a similar sentiment:

There is no dialogue [between the parties]. [. . .] "You are either in the blue team or the red team, and you never wander off. [. . .] And I never thought about it that much when I came, but it was very different then. It wasn't a parliamentary system, and people wandered off their side and voted in committee or on the floor with the other side. There was this understanding that we were there to solve problems.[4]

While some would extend such intractable rifts to the rest of the American people, this is simply not the case. Conventional wisdom assumes we are a nation of red states and blue states, a people evenly divided on almost every issue.

The truth is, Americans have achieved consensus on a number of issues relating to politics—not the least of which is our overwhelming agreement that politics has lost touch with the people, and the government should respect the principles we as a nation value most.

Days before the 2008 election, David Gergen and Andy Zelleke of the Center for Public Leadership at the Harvard Kennedy School of Government wrote in the *Christian Science Monitor*:

A startling 80 percent of the American people believe there is a leadership crisis in this country. In a nation so sharply divided on so many issues—politically and culturally—rare indeed is an 80 percent public consensus.[5]

That we have a consensus of 80, or even 90 percent, is not a terribly rare phenomenon. The issue of political polarization isn't a problem for most of us, yet for far too many politicians and pundits, we are all either red or blue. We may be a red-state voter in a blue state or a blue-state voter in a red state, but in the end we must pick one side or the other.

Perhaps this theory is right in one way: Poll after poll has shown that Americans are either feeling blue, or seeing red when it comes to politics.

A 2010 Washington Post-ABC News poll found two-thirds of Americans "dissatisfied" (48 percent) or downright "angry" (19 percent) about the way the federal government is working,[6] the highest percentage since 1996.[7] Similarly, in July 2010, a Gallup poll found only 11 percent of Americans have a great deal or quite a lot of confidence in Congress.[8] In fact, more people *volunteer* an answer choice not listed—that they have *no* confidence in Congress (five percent)—than choose to say they have "a great deal" of confidence in Congress (four percent).[9]

Our polling, too, has found a great deal of consensus. Eighty-two percent of Americans think politicians are moving the nation's moral compass in the wrong direction, more so than all other groups and sectors we compared them to such as religious leaders, public education, the news media and the entertainment industry.[10]

Likewise, by more than three to one (66 percent to 21 percent) Americans also see the federal government moving the moral compass of the country in the wrong direction. By more than two to one (60 percent to 25 percent) most Americans say the same of state and local governments.[11]

While Americans don't regard the judicial system quite as negatively as the political system, there is still concern. More Americans think judges are moving our nation's moral compass in the wrong direction (44 percent) than in the right direction (38 percent).[12]

Americans perceive a severe disconnect between themselves and their elected officials—and not just on political issues. As our polling has revealed, there is a moral component to their discontent as well.

The moral consensus of most Americans is real and transcends generations, races, economic classes and party lines. Somewhere in the political process, Americans' most deeply held values have been lost in translation.

In the summer of 2010, a poll commissioned by Politico highlighted the disconnect between the American public and Washington. Politico compared "D.C. elites" to Americans in general. The elites were defined as those who "live within the D.C. metro area, earn more than $75,000 per year, have at least a college degree and [are] involved in the political process or work on key political issues or policy decisions."[13]

The results were stunning. By more than a two to one ratio (61 percent to 27 percent) Americans see the country as heading in the wrong direction. D.C. elites, however, disagree. The plurality, 49 percent, think the country is on the right track, while only 45 percent agree with Americans that the nation is on the wrong one.[14]

Likewise, while the general population and Washington insiders are in agreement that D.C.'s political system is broken, the percentage of D.C. elites who do not see the system in need of being fixed, 31 percent, is more than twice the percentage of the general population that agrees (15 percent).[15]

Most telling though, was the poll's question on the importance of family values in the United States. Among the general population, more than six in 10 Americans (62 percent) say family values are "very important"—compared to less than a quarter (23 percent) of the Washington establishment who say likewise. In other words, there is a nearly 40-point difference between D.C. insiders and the rest of Americans over the belief that traditional family values have a prominent place in the national discussion. Only 14 percent of the general population thinks such values are not important, compared to 43 percent of Washington elites who would disregard them.[16]

"Politics," Otto von Bismark once said, "is the art of the possible." Americans would add that ethical politics is possible, too, but amid a seemingly endless series of political scandals—financial, legal, sexual and otherwise—they just don't see it as often as they would like in our political system today.

Our polling has found that a consensus—two-thirds of the country (66 percent)—believes politicians *can* be "ethical and successful," but only eight percent of Americans say political leaders are either "excellent" or "good" in honesty or ethical conduct. Nearly eight times that many Americans (62 percent) rate their honesty and ethics as poor. More than three-quarters of Americans (76 percent) regard politicians as rarely or never being guided by honesty and integrity in their political or policy-making decisions. Americans' impression of politicians' conduct in their personal lives is not much better: Sixty-six percent believe their political leaders seldom—if ever—live out the principles of honesty and integrity in their personal lives either.[17]

Gallup found that an increasing number of Americans wish the U.S. government would promote "traditional values"—53 percent in 2009, compared to 48 percent the year before[18]—and more than three-quarters (76 percent) believe America's moral values are getting worse.[19] It is little wonder we are witnessing palpable frustration over the disparity between Washington and the rest of the nation over the importance of morality and ethics.

In addition, the partisanship crisis that has left our political system at an impasse and Americans disillusioned with the effectiveness of government can be seen to have a moral component. The American people want values-based leadership. But a polarized political situation has little room for any common ground.

Several years ago, Sean Theriault of the University of Texas at Austin wrote a report titled, "The Case of the Vanishing Moderates: Party Polarization in the Modern Congress." He noted that there has been a shift toward partisanship since the 1960s. More recently, Theriault found an almost complete polarization of political parties and the disappearance of moderates. He observed:

In 1968, [. . .] over half (235) of all members were in the middle. In 1998, less than one-fifth (84) of all the members were in the middle third of the ideological continuum. During the same time period, the number of moderates in the Senate fell by more than 50 percent from 48 to 23.[20]

In a sign of our times, the recognition that the system is broken and plagued by factional rivalries has led to an increase in political candidates running against this status quo. All of our past three presidents have campaigned on such a transcendent platform.

For former President Bill Clinton, it was his "third way" as a "New Democrat."[21] For his successor, George W. Bush, it was the fact that he was "a uniter, not a divider."[22] For President Barack Obama, it was a promise to end the "partisanship and pettiness and immaturity that has poisoned our politics for so long."[23] None of the three has achieved his objective.

It is this political polarization that is then projected onto the rest of the country through talk of the so-called red state, blue state dichotomy. Politics has divided government, but it has united the rest of us in many ways: on the need for values in government, and on a host of moral, economic and political issues. It often feels like we aren't given much choice in changing things. We can vote for one party or the other, but in an era of monolithic party politics, it can seem like simply voting for a red brick or a blue brick in competing ramparts facing each other over the political no man's land of bipartisanship.

Unable to get the political system to work effectively, Americans have resorted to voting for gridlock. In the past 30 years, only in nine of those years has the president's party also held the majority in both House and Senate.[24]

Americans aren't the cause of the polarity. They are the victims of it, as the moral center of America evaporates into the left and right wings of politics the moment it sends someone to represent it in an elected body.

This data, combined with the even poorer moral regard in which we hold our politicians, in no small part explains why we don't have much faith in government and view it as having lost touch with something that Americans have always placed above government— moral values.

A discussion on what Americans are looking for in government— and in what areas they think government is overstepping its role— will be most productive if it considers the historical context of how America has viewed the role of government from the very beginning.

There, one will find that for the men who declared their independence from England on July 4, 1776, the rights they claimed were not a human creation, but were—and continue to be— bestowed by their Creator. This is the American ideal: that there is something above the state—something that transcends government—that is an objective moral order against which the actions of men will be judged.

Even when a government denies those rights—as the British government did to its colonists in the 18th century, or as the Confederacy did to a full third of its population in the 19th century—Americans understood, as they still do, that their rights existed regardless of their government's willingness, or unwillingness, to protect them.

Two years before drafting the Declaration of Independence, in preparation for the first Continental Congress, the future President Thomas Jefferson wrote a short treatise titled "A Summary View of the Rights of British America." In it, he argued that a free people claims their rights "as derived from the laws of nature, and not as the gift of their chief magistrate."[25]

In 1863 at Gettysburg, President Abraham Lincoln invoked the Declaration with his stirring exhortation for the United States to endure—"that this nation under God shall have a new birth of freedom, and that government of the people, by the people, for the people shall not perish from the earth."[26]

A century later, at the peak of the Cold War, President John F. Kennedy continued this theme in his inaugural address when he noted that the Founders of our country had fought for the belief that our rights came from God rather than the state.[27]

Likewise, from a Birmingham jail a few years later, Reverend Martin Luther King, Jr. wrote that civil rights protesters were bringing the country back to the "best in the American dream," in keeping with the religious values that were the foundation of our nation.[28]

Most Americans, 58 percent, still agree with the Declaration of Independence's affirmation that mankind's inalienable rights are "endowed by their Creator."[29] Presidents Jefferson, Lincoln and Kennedy and Reverend King might wish the number to be higher, but the idea that our rights spring from a place above the government continues to resonate with most Americans. This, it seems, is what we have remembered, and what politics has largely forgotten.

Americans believe that there is something higher than government. The American people have never wanted a nation in which the government tries to do everything. We are a nation whose Constitution is based on the principle of shared, representative government that is given its power by the people. In turn, that government reserves for the people and the states those powers it has not been given. In the words of Ronald Reagan, "We are a nation that has a government—not the other way around."[30]

Americans continue to hold a deep reverence for our constitutional principles. An AP-National Constitution Center poll found that 75 percent of Americans believe the Constitution is both enduring and relevant today.[31] In our own poll, a majority of Americans, 56 percent, say they think the Constitution should be applied "exactly as it is written," rather than reinterpreted for time and circumstance.[32]

The problem is that Americans today don't see our government as responsive to the will of the people. Rasmussen has found that only 23 percent of voters nationwide believe the federal government is functioning with the consent of the governed.[33] Additionally, more than two-thirds of voters (68 percent) say the political class doesn't care what most Americans think.[34] It's a statement that seems supported by Politico's findings on the disconnect between Washington elites and most Americans.

What polling reveals is that Americans—while currently lacking confidence in the government's ability to solve problems such as the economic crisis or flaws in the immigration system—want an effective yet limited government that promotes the nation's foundational values, rather than erodes them.

Consider the political situation today regarding immigration. In a nation where 64 percent say respect for the law is undervalued, it should not come as a surprise that illegal immigration does not enjoy popular support.[35]

In May 2010, during the immediate aftermath of Arizona's controversial law clamping down on illegal immigrants within the state, a poll from Quinnipiac University found 59 percent of Americans consider illegal immigration a "very serious" problem in the United States. An additional 26 percent said it was "somewhat serious."[36]

Americans want the rule of law upheld and see it proper to the role of government to ensure this. Multiple polls have shown a majority of Americans in support of Arizona's immigration law, as well as a super-consensus in the nation that the current U.S. immigration system is profoundly broken.[37] In fact, according to Lake Research Partners, a majority of those in favor of Arizona's law, 52 percent, support it because "the federal government has failed to solve the problem." Only 28 percent favor the law because they be-lieve "it will reduce illegal immigration."[38]

However, when pressed further on their views on immigration, it's clear that Americans also express concern for the wellbeing of immigrants themselves. Despite anxiety over the issue of illegal im-migration, our polling showed that the overwhelming consensus among Americans, 77 percent, is that most illegal immigrants are ordinary people who "come to the United States seeking a better life for themselves and their families."[39]

Americans agree that there is a dire need for immigration re-form,[40] but that doesn't mean they see the choice as either border security or immigrant rights. They strongly believe that immigra-tion laws can both secure the nation's borders and extend respect to immigrants themselves. By nearly four to one (79 percent to 21 percent), we found Americans think both ideals are attainable.[41]

According to a CNN poll in May 2010, eight in 10 Americans would favor a program that would allow illegal immigrants already within the U.S. for a number of years to stay and apply for perma-nent residence as long as they were employed and paid back taxes.[42]

Ironically, this is one area in which Americans, who otherwise tend to be wary of federal action, would like to see the govern-ment step in and devise a sensible and fair solution to the issue. As the politics of any proposed solution is debated, Americans find themselves again disappointed—this time, by government's lack of action.

Our desire to uphold the rule of law—and frustration over what we see as government inaction to do so—does not preclude sympa-thy toward those seeking a better life within our borders.

The economy is another obvious case that reflects Americans' views on the role of government. A July 2010 Washington Post-ABC News poll found that nine in 10 Americans have a negative outlook on the state of the nation's economy.[42] Our own survey, too, has found Americans to be extremely worried about our economic future and doubtful that Washington will be able to fix the problem. Our polling in January 2010 showed that a majority of Americans, 59 percent, were not confident that solutions to the country's economic downturn can come from Washington, D.C.[43] By July, that number had risen to 70 percent.[44]

But Americans do want their elected officials—or those whom they will elect—to try in one area in particular. Asked what political positions would encourage them to vote for a candidate, commitment to make job creation the top priority came in at number one, with 96 percent of Americans saying this would win their vote.[45]

Still, despite their wish for politicians who will approach the current crisis with effective solutions, Americans remain doubtful that the current state of politics will foster true recovery.

Even in the midst of "the great recession" that began in the financial services sector of the economy, we found that a majority of Americans, 55 percent, believe "more government regulation will hurt business and the economy."[46]

Tellingly, a Gallup poll in 2009 found most Americans believe "big government" was a greater threat to the future of the country than "big business" by a sizable margin of 55 percent to 32 percent.[47] Similarly, an AP-Constitution Center poll found that three in four Americans oppose expanding the power of the presidency even if doing so improved the economy, while almost as many, 71 percent, oppose letting the federal government take partial ownership of private companies to prevent them from going out of business.[48]

In fact, despite the ethical problems Americans see in the business community, they don't see the government as offering a viable solution. In 2009, a Rasmussen poll found 70 percent of Americans feel that—far from reining in abuses—big government and big business are on the same team against the interests of both consumers and investors. This sentiment is shared by Americans regardless of their race, age, ideology or political party.[49]

Consistent with their concern about the efficacy of government policies, Americans are lukewarm toward more government involvement in the health care system.[50] Months after the passage of the most significant government health care plan in years, Americans remain unconvinced that this act alone will solve the problems in our health care system. In August 2010, Rasmussen found that nearly six in 10 Americans favor the repeal of health care legislation, consistent with their findings since the bill's passage in March 2010, which have shown that a majority—fluctuating from 51 to 60 percent—is against the legislation.[51] A CBS poll the same month found that only 13 percent feel the new health care law will help them personally, while over twice as many think it will hurt them.[52]

We asked Americans whom they trust most to make health care decisions on their behalf. Ninety-five percent say either their doctor (61 percent) or their family (34 percent). Almost no one (just over one percent) points to the government.[53]

Despite the worries of authors like Daniel Callahan,[54] who advocates for age-based restrictions on certain care due to costs and resource allocation, and despite the concerns of politicians and insurance companies about balancing costs with saving lives, almost all Americans—more than nine in 10—think a "health insurance plan should cover everyone at the same level of health care, regardless of age or health." Those who would limit health care for the sick or elderly in order to manage costs find themselves with support only in the single digits (eight percent).[55]

On the issue of health care, as elsewhere, Americans want the better angels of our nature to be heeded. They don't want to bind up the wounds of one group and leave others to suffer without care. With health care—as with other issues surveyed—they want a universal moral compass to guide policy.

Table 1: Influence People or Institutions Have on the Moral Direction of the Country

	Right Direction	Wrong Direction	No Effect
Volunteers	73%	5%	22%
Charitable organizations	61%	15%	24%
The U.S. military	55%	24%	21%
Private education	55%	22%	23%
Law enforcement	51%	30%	19%
Families	50%	36%	14%
Doctors	50%	20%	30%
Religious values	48%	35%	17%
Scientists	47%	26%	27%
Religious leaders	43%	38%	19%
Public education	40%	46%	14%
Judges	37%	44%	19%
The Internet	27%	52%	21%
Your state or local government	25%	60%	15%
Federal government	21%	66%	13%
Lawyers	21%	59%	20%
News media	18%	68%	14%
Professional athletes	17%	62%	21%
Business executives	15%	63%	22%
Immigrants	15%	59%	26%
Entertainment industry	13%	73%	14%
Politicians	10%	82%	8%

Do you think each of the following people or institutions are mostly moving the moral compass of this country in the right direction, the wrong direction or have no effect?

The Knights of Columbus/Marist Poll July 2010 Survey

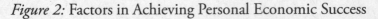

Figure 2: Factors in Achieving Personal Economic Success

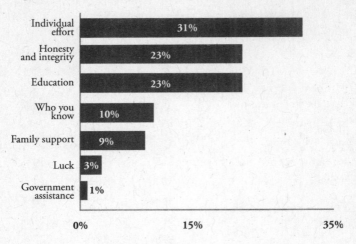

Which one of the following do you think is most valuable in achieving personal economic success?

The Knights of Columbus/Marist Poll July 2010 Survey

Lack of faith that government knows best is evident in other sectors such as education. For instance, while 55 percent of Americans think private education is moving the country's moral compass in the right direction, only 40 percent say the same about public education.[56]

On a personal level, even though members of both parties have supported some form of economic regulation and stimulus, Americans have very little faith that government will help them achieve economic success. We asked Americans what they believe to be the most important factors in attaining this goal. Government finished last at slightly more than one percent, just below sheer "luck."[57] On the other hand, more than three-quarters of Americans identify three personal choices as the best ways to succeed financially: individual effort (31 percent), honesty and integrity (23 percent), and education (23 percent). Americans look to themselves—not government—to help them achieve economic success.

Similarly, when we asked Americans where they look for guidance in life, less than one in five indicate that they looked to government "a great deal" or "a good amount." Even "business" did better. Instead, vast majorities of Americans say they look to family (86 percent) and religion (63 percent).[58]

Figure 3: Trust to Spend Americans' Money

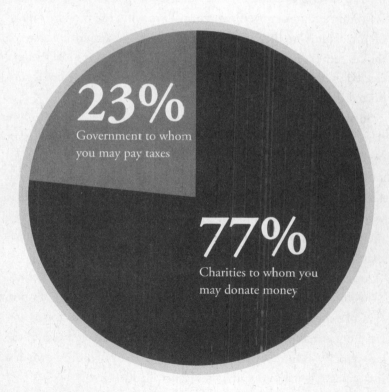

Do you trust that your money is better spent by:

The Knights of Columbus/Marist Poll July 2010 Survey

This would probably not surprise those like President George Washington, who called religion and morality "indispensable supports"[59] of the American political system; Alexis de Tocqueville, who was struck by the American way of uniting "the spirit of religion and the spirit of freedom";[60] or President John F. Kennedy, who reminded us of the source of our rights.

Such views are the consensus in America. It is a tragedy that in the 21st century Americans have lost faith in our institutions.

We see "big government" as problematic, not only because of Americans' longstanding, historical consensus for limited government, but also because of our overwhelming agreement that federal, state and local governments are all moving the moral compass of the nation in the "wrong direction."[61] We Americans have a moral sense that transcends partisan politics, but most believe elected officials don't share that ethical sense, and that belief is supported by polls of Washington's elites.

So who is getting it right? Only two groups are cited by more than 60 percent of Americans as moving the nation's moral compass in the right direction: charitable organizations (61 percent) and volunteers (73 percent). In an economic crisis caused by greed, Americans are looking to altruism—to love of neighbor—as the way forward. Nearly three in four Americans (73 percent) believe their money is better spent by the charities to which they donate, than by the governments to which they pay taxes.[62]

Americans have made this country the world's most generous. Two-thirds of Americans donate to charity. By contrast, only 15 percent of Americans participate in a government, political or issue-related organization.[63] Twice as many say they volunteered within the past year[64]—a number that grows to more than two-thirds when a list of possible volunteer activities is provided.[65]

Americans value hard work, personal initiative, generosity and the role of religious and moral values in public life. While it's not unexpected that concern over unemployment tops Americans' priorities in terms of what they look for in a political candidate, the next position they consider important might take several by surprise: the promise to uphold religious liberty and freedom of conscience. More than nine in 10 (92 percent) Americans say they would vote for a candidate who makes this a priority—a testament to the nation's enduring sense that freedom of religion must always be protected.[66]

Far from a partisan wasteland, America has a strong moral consensus as its people look to their families and faith-based values for guidance. It's a compass that can serve as politicians' roadmap to effective governing—if they are willing to set aside partisanship and agree to meet where the American people already stand. Americans' values are not hard to pinpoint—one need only listen.

5

Beyond the Clash
of Absolutes: Abortion

The title of Harvard Law professor Laurence Tribe's 1992 book, *Abortion: The Clash of Absolutes*, is perhaps the best summation of the manner in which abortion is usually portrayed in the United States.

"Our national institutions are braced for a seemingly endless clash of absolutes," Tribe wrote. "The political stage is already dominated by the well-rehearsed and deeply felt arguments, on either side of the abortion issue, that we have come to know so well. The debate is unending."[1]

There is the sense that the subject is irreconcilable, and that consensus can only be found on the fringes of the debate, in peripheral areas such as prenatal care or adoption. The possibility that Americans could ever agree on broader abortion legislation is seen as extremely unlikely.

Leaders of both our political parties speak of abortion in a similar way. For example, in August 2000, at the Republican National Convention, the soon-to-be elected George W. Bush said the following:

I know good people disagree on this issue, but surely we can agree on ways to value life by promoting adoption and parental notification, and when Congress sends me a bill against partial-birth abortion, I will sign it into law.[2]

Similarly, nearly a decade later, speaking at The University of Notre Dame in 2009, President Barack Obama said this:

> So let us work together to reduce the number of women seeking abortions, let's reduce unintended pregnancies. Let's make adoption more available. Let's provide care and support for women who do carry their children to term.

He added:

> I do not suggest that the debate surrounding abortion can or should go away. Because no matter how much we may want to fudge it—indeed, while we know that the views of most Americans on the subject are complex and even contradictory—the fact is that at some level, the views of the two camps are irreconcilable.[3]

Pollsters, too, usually see the issue as intractable. In 2008, John Zogby wrote that we had to think through the public's contradictions on the abortion issue to move past the ongoing "intractability that has plagued the abortion discussion since *Roe v. Wade.*"[4]

The idea is that we need to find a way forward, but that none currently exists. For commentators including Tribe, the only way forward would be for the polarized halves of the American people to move toward the center.[5] Somewhere along the way, the terms "pro-choice" and "pro-life" were taken as monolithic and applied, all or nothing, to every American. Polls that asked Americans to choose one label or the other lent credence to this apparent division.

We have seen the focus on the "number wars" in abortion polling played out with the conventional understanding over the past two years. The "deep divide" among Americans over abortion made headlines once again in 2009 after Gallup reported a slight change in the direction of the polarity: For the first time since Gallup began asking the question in 1995, Americans—who had long identified themselves by narrow margins as pro-choice—now responded that they were pro-life, 51 to 42 percent.[6]

Soon, other polls confirmed this. For many covering the slight shift in the winds, the ongoing story was the continued polarity. When the Pew Research Center's 2009 poll likewise found the public slowly moving away from supporting abortion, *The New York Times* covered it this way: "A new poll, though, suggests that support for abortion may have declined, with the public almost evenly divided over the issue."[7] A few months later, when the Gallup poll found the gap had tightened (now with 47 percent pro-life vs. 46 percent pro-choice), the *U.S. News & World Report* "God and Country" blog declared "Americans Evenly Split on Abortion."[8]

While the lead remained close, the momentum, it seemed, was with pro-life Americans—but only by single digits.

Even so, more than three decades after *Roe v. Wade*, and with two political parties so identified with opposing stances on abortion, this was big news. Like a World Cup match in overtime, the smallest point-advantage was significant. This was seen to such an extent that in 2010, when the narrow lead among those identifying as pro-life still held, Gallup declared "the new normal on abortion."[9]

Conventional wisdom holds that, as with a World Cup match, the only constant is this: Regardless of which side holds a slight advantage, the two will always be almost evenly matched competitors. The numbers might vary by a few percentage points, but—so the story goes—Americans will always be split between two rival and antithetical positions.

Even these small shifts were sometimes dismissed as simply political. As Gallup itself explained in 2010:

> Barring evidence that Americans are growing more wary about the morality of abortion per se, the trends by party identification suggest that increased political polarization may be a factor in Republicans' preference for the "pro-life" label, particularly since Barack Obama

took office. Whatever the cause, the effect is that the "pro-life" label has become increasingly dominant among Republicans and to a lesser degree among independents, while the "pro-choice" label has become more dominant among Democrats.[10]

Such commentary suggests that Americans care more about political candidates than they do about abortion itself, and that abortion has become an issue linked more to partisan affiliation than to personal opinion on the issue.

One could easily conclude, as Tribe does, that "the debate is unending." But Americans want it to end. Nearly four decades after *Roe v. Wade*, 82 percent of Americans say the argument on abortion has gone on for too long.[11] Far from wishful thinking, Americans' desire to see the debate resolved is closer to reality than the idea of a country evenly divided between absolute positions on the issue.

There is consensus, enormous consensus, on abortion among Americans—that is, if you give people more choice in responding to surveys on the issue.

Pollsters often ask if people support all, some, few or no abortions. However, understanding that induced abortion is a procedure than can only happen during pregnancy, and that pregnancy is divided into gestational periods (trimesters), we decided to poll based on the terms used in the medical and legal professions. As it turns out, asking Americans to consider abortion in terms of these clearly defined time periods within a pregnancy yielded very interesting answers.

We found that about eight out of 10 Americans (84 percent in 2008, 86 percent in 2009, 79 percent in 2010) favor restrictions that would limit abortion to the first three months of pregnancy at most.[12]

We didn't find a clash of absolutes but a consensus on what almost everyone sees as the most hopelessly divisive issue in America today.

Figure 1: Spectrum of Opinion on Abortion

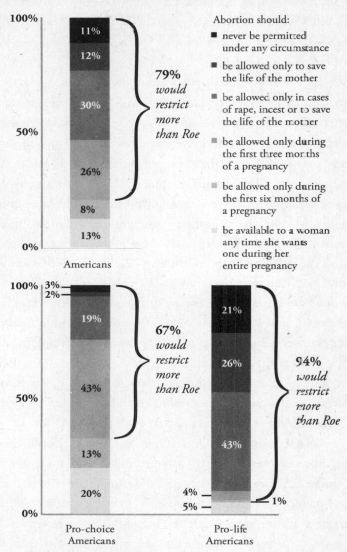

Abortion should:
- never be permitted under any circumstance
- be allowed only to save the life of the mother
- be allowed only in cases of rape, incest or to save the life of the mother
- be allowed only during the first three months of a pregnancy
- be allowed only during the first six months of a pregnancy
- be available to a woman any time she wants one during her entire pregnancy

Which one of the following statements comes closest to your opinion on abortion?

The Knights of Columbus/Marist Poll July 2010 Survey

Even within this overwhelming consensus, the majority favors more restriction rather than less. Fifty-three percent of Americans would limit abortion to cases of rape, incest or to save the life of a mother—or would not allow it at all. Among women, the number is even higher—55 percent.[13]

The clash of absolutes is actually hard to find. Less than a quarter of Americans choose an absolute position: Fourteen percent want abortion allowed at any time during a pregnancy and 11 percent believe abortion should never be permitted under any circumstances.[14] Whatever "pro-" label people say they identify with, in the area of legislation, almost all Americans fall into a category somewhere between the two absolute positions, with the overwhelming majority united in their agreement that abortion should be restricted far more than it is now. That moral consensus—that abortion can and should be restricted—ought to be the starting point for resolving the political impasse on abortion.

We don't need to move the two polarized halves of the American population toward a compromise position on abortion; we need to start our conversation in the place where the overwhelming majority of Americans already stand.

In addition to our own polling, other polls that have offered respondents a wider spectrum of possible answers have likewise seen a consensus in favor of significant restriction of abortion.

In April 2010, a poll from CNN/Opinion Research Corporation asked Americans nationwide, "Do you think abortion should be legal under any circumstances, legal only under certain circumstances, or illegal in all circumstances?" Seventy-eight percent favored abortion only under certain circumstances or never at all, with only 21 percent selecting legal abortion under any circumstances. The CNN poll then went even further, asking those who responded "legal under only certain circumstances" whether abortions should be allowed in most cases, or only a few. As in our poll, an increase in options resulted in a noticeable trend among respondents in favor of significant restriction on abortion. By a more than three to one ratio, Americans—given such options—say that abortion should be legal in only a few circumstances.[15]

Interestingly, women are actually likelier to favor more stringent restrictions than men. While 16 percent of men say abortion should be legal any time, only 11 percent of women say the same. A slightly higher percentage of women would restrict abortion completely: Thirteen percent of women say abortion should never be permitted under any circumstance compared to nine percent of men.[16]

In other words, not only would more women completely restrict abortion than allow it at any time during the pregnancy, but the consensus for restricting abortion in general is even higher among women than among men: Eighty-two percent of women and 76 percent of men want abortion restricted to—at most—the first three months of pregnancy.[17]

It's a trend that's not likely to change.

A 2005 Zogby poll of high school seniors—an age cohort comprising those who were, or were about to become, the nation's youngest voters, and thus those with the most elections still ahead of them—found that young people have reached a consensus on abortion.

Seventy percent of female students say they wouldn't consider an abortion themselves, and 67 percent of male students wouldn't want their girlfriend to have an abortion.[18] Additionally, while the poll listed six possible rationales for abortion, a majority of students support it only in cases of serious threats to the mother's health and in cases of pregnancy resulting from rape.[19]

Though the broad consensus for significant abortion restriction has not received much attention, some have noticed the youthful trend toward the pro-life position.

"I just thought, my gosh, they are so young," Nancy Keenan, president of NARAL Pro-Choice America, said when she surveyed the crowd at the pro-life "March for Life" in Washington, D.C. "There are so many of them, and they are so young."[20]

Young people are increasingly pro-life. Fifty-six percent of the general population believes abortion is morally wrong, an opinion that resonates in strong majorities across age demographics. This includes nearly six in 10 "Millennials" (58 percent). Sixty percent of those in "Generation X" and 62 percent of those who make up the "Silent," and "Greatest" generation agreed, as did a majority of "Baby Boomers" (51 percent).[21]

In addition, two-thirds of students in the Zogby poll (67 percent) said abortion was wrong—either always (23 percent) or usually (44 percent). By contrast, only four percent said abortion was always right.[22]

The lesson here is not that there is a small shift to the overall "pro-life" label, but that the trend and consensus—which include so many young people—is stable for the foreseeable future.

Some commentators have a difficult time reconciling statistics like these. As the Hamilton College commentary on the Zogby poll of high school students noted:

> Many high school students are not strangers to this issue. Half the females and 36 percent of the males polled say they know someone who has had an abortion. We asked females whether they would "consider" abortion if they became pregnant in high school and males whether they would want their partner to do so. The response from 70 percent of females and 67 percent of males was "No." However, the relatively high proportions of seniors who know someone who has had an abortion suggests they might themselves be more open to it if faced with a real decision about their own lives and futures.[23]

But the logic—and numbers—of the last statement in this commentary just don't add up. In 2005, when this poll was conducted, less than 30 percent of 16- to 18-year-old girls who became pregnant ended their pregnancy by having an abortion.[24] In other words, while 70 percent of the students responding to Zogby's poll said hypothetically they would not consider an abortion. Reality was consistent with this. By an almost identical margin, more than 70 percent of their classmates who actually were pregnant chose not to have an abortion.

The fact that even more women in the general population have had abortions hasn't made abortion any more popular. The Guttmacher Institute estimates that one in three women will have an abortion at some point in their lives.[25] Even if that number is high, it means that many of us are likely to know someone who has had an abortion. Perhaps it is for that very reason that Americans by more than a two to one margin don't think abortion solves problems in the long term. By 53 to 26 percent, most believe that "abortion does more harm than good," rather than "improve a woman's life."[26]

The anguishing factors that lead many women to feel that abortion is their only choice are real—even the partisans agree on that. However, the American people know that whatever abortion may seem to "fix" in the short term, it's much more complicated than that in the weeks, months and years following the loss of a child.[27]

Legally speaking, the consensus on abortion is reflected also in Americans' understanding of the things that laws should prohibit and those that laws should protect.

For instance, when asked if laws can protect both the health of the mother and the life of her unborn child, 81 percent of Americans say yes—including 74 percent of those who identify as pro-choice.[28]

Asked if health care workers or doctors should be required to perform or assist with abortions despite their religious or moral objections, 79 percent of Americans answer no. They want the law to protect freedom of conscience. Again, two-thirds (67 percent) of those who identify themselves as pro-choice also feel this way.[29]

With such a widespread agreement on limiting abortion, this consensus has had an impact on other debates as well. During the

Figure 2: Views on Abortion

Which statement comes closer to your view?

	Americans	Pro-life Americans	Pro-choice Americans
It is possible to have laws which protect both the health and well-being of a woman and the life of the unborn	81%	89%	74%
It is necessary for laws to choose to protect one and not the other	19%	11%	26%

The Knights of Columbus/Marist Poll July 2010 Survey

Do you think health care workers such as doctors and nurses who believe abortion is wrong should be required to perform them, or not?

	Americans	Pro-life Americans	Pro-choice Americans
Yes, required	21%	8%	33%
No	79%	92%	67%

The Knights of Columbus/Marist Poll July 2009 Survey

In the long run, do you believe having an abortion improves a woman's life or in the long run, do you believe abortion does more harm than good to a woman?

	Americans	Pro-life Americans	Pro-choice Americans
Improves a woman's life	26%	7%	45%
Does more harm than good	53%	85%	23%
Does not make a difference	3%	1%	5%
Unsure	18%	7%	27%

The Knights of Columbus/Marist Poll July 2009 Survey

2009-2010 health care debate, Americans rejected the inclusion of abortion coverage in federally funded plans by a similar percentage of more than six in 10.[30]

In his book *The Way We'll Be*, John Zogby noted of abortion views that, "as amazing as it seems, we appear to be arriving at what amounts to a national conversation on such a divisive subject."[31] Perhaps we should add that this conversation has resulted in an overwhelming consensus—a consensus in favor of significant restriction of abortion beyond those currently in place in the United States. Those in positions of political or judicial leadership should have the courage to go beyond the high-profile polarities and listen to the results of our "national conversation," using this consensus as its starting point—even if a small percentage of the country disagrees.

How did we arrive at a place where eight in 10 Americans favor restricting abortion to the first three months of pregnancy—a tighter restriction than can be construed from any possible reading of *Roe v. Wade*?

To understand how America finds itself with the abortion laws it has today, it is important to review both pivotal court cases that legalized elective abortion: *Roe v. Wade* and *Doe v. Bolton*. On its face, *Roe* seems to allow state legislatures to ban abortion in the third trimester. Indeed, according to the Guttmacher Institute, 38 states have some form of this third trimester restriction in place, counting either from 24 weeks or from viability (which generally occurs at about 24 weeks).[32]

However, such restrictions are illusory. In his opinion in the *Roe* case, Justice Harry Blackmun insisted that *Roe* must be "read together" with *Doe v. Bolton*,[33] a companion case that was handed down on the same day. *Doe* also challenged the abortion laws, with the result that "health of the mother" was more loosely defined. As Justice Blackmun explained it:

> The medical judgment may be exercised in light of all factors—phys-ical, emotional, psychological, familial, and the woman's age—rele-vant to the well-being of the patient. All these factors may relate to health. This allows the attending physician the room he needs to make his best medical judgment. And it is room that operates for the benefit, not the disadvantage, of the pregnant woman.[34]

In other words, in *Doe*, the health of the mother was so broadly defined—to include not just the life of the mother but her quality of life—that it swallowed up any possibility of a real restriction on late-term abortions, as promised by *Roe*. What the Court gave, the Court took away, and practically speaking, abortion could no longer be restricted.

Additionally, in most cases, the one making the decision about the mother's health is also a person with a financial stake in the de-cision, and *Doe* can easily be used to assert that health makes an abortion necessary even in the most dubious of cases.[35]

This is a legacy that sits well with only a fraction of Americans.

People on both sides of the aisle recognize the problems of Supreme Court jurisprudence on abortion. One of those who has spoken publicly on this issue is Supreme Court Justice Ruth Bader Ginsburg, who addressed students at Princeton University in 2008. Her speech was summarized as follows:

> On *Roe v. Wade*, which was decided in 1973, Ginsburg reiterated her previous criticism of the ruling. A strong supporter of abortion rights, Ginsburg nevertheless said the court "bit off more than it could chew." A more incremental decision "would have been an

opportunity for a dialogue with the state legislators" and a chance for states to take the lead on the issue.[36]

Her statement doesn't sound too different from that of Clarke, Forsythe, senior counsel of Americans United for Life, who wrote in his book *Politics for the Greatest Good: The Case for Prudence in the Public Square*:

> The Supreme Court's 1973 decision in *Roe v. Wade* was an unnecessary, unconstitutional and tragic decision. It abruptly silenced a vigorous national debate that was ongoing among the American people, across the states. It overturned the abortion laws of all fifty states, most of which were actively enforced and many of which had been recently debated, enacted or reaffirmed by the people of the state. [. . .]·
>
> With *Roe*, the Supreme Court incurred a self-inflicted wound. It did not understand the history of abortion: while the Court spent half of its opinion trying to base its decision in history, virtually all of its historical propositions have been thoroughly discredited over the past three decades. It did not understand the legal context of its ruling: the states have regularly passed laws since *Roe* that have increased legal protection for the unborn outside the context of abortion (fetal homicide laws). And it did not foresee the negative public reaction to its decision that has been sustained over three decades.[37]

The problems were apparent, even in the months immediately following the *Roe* decision. John Hart Ely, a professor of law at Harvard University and a specialist in constitutional law—himself prochoice—had this to say in 1973 about the legal reasoning of *Roe*:

> It is nevertheless a very bad decision. Not because it will perceptibly weaken the Court—it won't; and not because it conflicts with either my idea of progress or what the evidence suggests is society's—it doesn't. It is bad because it is bad constitutional law, or rather because

it is not constitutional law and gives almost no sense of an obligation to try to be. [. . .] What is unusual about *Roe* is that the liberty involved is accorded a far more stringent protection, so stringent that a desire to preserve the fetus's existence is unable to overcome it—a protection more stringent, I think it fair to say, than that the present Court accords the freedom of the press explicitly guaranteed by the First Amendment. What is frightening about *Roe* is that this super-protected right is not inferable from the language of the Constitution, the framers' thinking respecting the specific problem in issue, any general value derivable from the provisions they included, or the nation's governmental structure. Nor is it explainable in terms of the unusual political impotence of the group judicially protected vis-à-vis the interest that legislatively prevailed over it. And that, I believe— the predictable early reaction to *Roe* notwithstanding [. . .]—is a charge that can responsibly be leveled at no other decision of the past twenty years. At times the inferences the Court has drawn from the values the Constitution marks for special protection have been controversial, even shaky, but never before has its sense of an obligation to draw one been so obviously lacking.[38]

It wasn't just that *Roe* was out of step with the Constitution, but its legacy has proved out of step with the rest of the world as well. The abortion regime it ushered in is literally one of the world's most permissive. In her 1987 book *Abortion and Divorce in Western Law*, Harvard law professor Mary Ann Glendon made the case that nowhere else in the Western world is abortion less regulated than in the United States. As she put it:

When American abortion law is viewed in comparative perspective, it presents several unique features. Not only do we have less regulation of abortion in the interest of the fetus than any other Western nation, but we provide less public support for maternity and child raising. And to a greater extent than in any other country, our courts have shut down the legislative process of bargaining, education, and persuasion on the abortion issue.[39]

This is not simply an issue of the American people needing to catch up to the progressive foresight of the Supreme Court. Consider the difference in the public reaction toward another controversial issue: desegregation. In 1954, the Supreme Court's ruling against school segregation in *Brown v. Board of Education* resonated across America. At the time, a majority of Americans approved of the decision, but not overwhelmingly. Yet within the first few years after the Court's ruling, opinion began to change. By the end of 1956, Americans approved of the ruling in *Brown* by more than two to one. By the mid-1990s, Americans had overwhelmingly embraced the legacy of the Court's decision.[40]

I saw this clear consensus for myself while serving for nearly a decade as a member of the U.S. Commission on Civil Rights in 1990s, when I had the chance to gauge the support of the American public for *Brown v. Board of Education.* Clearly, *Brown* resonated with fundamental American principles of equality, fairness and freedom—something that was evident to me in my work for the commission in cities from coast to coast.

Contrast this embrace of *Brown's* legacy with public opinion toward *Roe v. Wade.* When the decision was made in 1973, polling—without the number of choices ours had—showed that, at best, scarcely 20 percent of Americans believed abortion should be legal under any circumstances.[41] However, abortion under any circumstances is exactly what has come to define *Roe's* legacy through subsequent Court rulings, legislation and aggressive advocacy. Today, abortion under any circumstances is no more popular than it was in 1973, and in fact that viewpoint is one of the smallest groups within our polling data at 14 percent. Thirty-seven years after *Roe v. Wade,* the Court's ruling has failed to garner consensus among the American people. *Roe v. Wade* was a rush to judgment that, unlike *Brown*, was significantly out of step with the moral sense of the American people.

There is an important lesson for both sides in all this. Each of us, too, has a role to play in helping ensure that no one feels an abortion is the only choice. No one puts abortion on her list of life goals—it's an act in desperate circumstances. But that makes it even more imperative that all of us—of whatever political persuasion—pursue solutions so that women do not feel they are in a situation where their only "option" is an abortion—which most Americans believe is neither a moral choice nor the best one.

As I related in my first book, *A Civilization of Love*, the truth of this was brought home to me and my wife in a very personal way. We learned that the daughter of a mutual friend had become pregnant soon after graduating from high school. She didn't want an abortion, but at the same time she didn't want to face her friends and neighbors. We invited this young woman to live with us. We were able to find her a job, and during the time of her pregnancy she became part of our family. Both my wife and I were deeply impressed by her courage and her dedication to her child. Women in difficult circumstances deserve a helping hand, not just rhetoric about abortion.[42]

' Understanding that abortion is a moral issue with serious, practical, and life-changing implications, the personal element is shown in who Americans want to hear from regarding the abortion issue. On a scale of 1-5, with 5 being very interested, more than half of Americans (53 percent) want very much to hear from a woman who has had an abortion. Only one out of four do not. Compare this to 66 percent (or two-thirds) of Americans who do *not* want to hear from a politician on the issue.[43]

Considering abortion a moral issue, a consensus of nearly seven in 10 Americans believe it is proper for religious leaders to speak out on abortion, and nearly six in 10 say religious leaders have a key role to play in the national debate on the issue.[44]

Washington, De Tocqueville, Lincoln and Kennedy—to name just a few—had faith in the United States as a moral and religious country. So did Harriet Tubman, who often invoked God in her work.

Writing from a jail in Birmingham, Reverend Martin Luther King, Jr. would note that those who protested against segregated lunch counters were bringing the nation back to the Judeo Christian roots of its founding.[45]

Reverend King—as with so many key figures in American history—was unwilling to believe that his religious conviction disqualified him from speaking out. No one today believes he made the wrong choice. Americans on this issue as well don't want to be told that certain rationales are disqualified.

Americans are happy to support those related issues "we can all agree on"—adoption, prenatal care and finding ways to assist pregnant women in need. But they can also agree on substantial change to our nation's core abortion laws.

The idea that our country is divided on restricting abortion is a myth, and justifications for avoiding the issue on that basis no longer apply. The goals can be achieved. We must only find those in the courts, politics and the media with the courage to move in that direction, and as a nation with a broad consensus, we must demand that they do so.

The vast majority of the American people have a vision in which abortion is talked about in moral terms, where it is restricted— with broad support, with consensus achieved. They look forward to an America whose abortion laws are not the most radical in the Western world, whose debate is not stifled by appeals to a Supreme Court decision. The American people have moved beyond the abortion impasse. What is needed now is the right combination of political leadership and courage.

6

Beyond Mythology:
The Statistics of Marriage

If there is "common knowledge" about how Americans view marriage today, it is this: Those who marry can be almost evenly divided into two groups of similar size—those whose marriages succeed and those whose marriages end in divorce.

Compared to the 1950s, cohabitation is more common, as is single parenthood. Divorce no longer seems taboo, and as a nation we are debating the very meaning of marriage itself.

As a result, many people seem to think that the demise of marriage—or its irrelevancy—is at hand. One articulation of this argument came in the *Newsweek* article "I Don't: The Case Against Marriage," in June 2010. In it, authors Jessica Bennett and Jesse Ellison challenged the efficacy of marriage today:

Once upon a time, marriage made sense. It was how women ensured their financial security, got the fathers of their children to stick around, and gained access to a host of legal rights. But 40 years after the feminist movement established our rights in the workplace, a generation after the divorce rate peaked, and a decade after *Sex and the City* made singledom chic, marriage is—from a legal and practical standpoint, anyway—no longer necessary. . . . [H]appily ever after doesn't have to include "I do."[1]

Even many of our cultural cues often seem to portray marriage in a less-than-important light. From television shows like *The Bachelor* and *Bridezillas*, which sensationalize and trivialize getting married, to *Divorce Court*, which trivializes ending marriages, to the steady stream of highly publicized celebrity marital woes, many of our cultural indicators seem to emphasize the skeptical view that marriage can be nothing more than an endeavor with a break-even chance of success in any particular instance.

Consider the dire picture of marriage painted by Gerry Kreyche in his *USA Today* article titled "The Demise of Marriage":

> Las Vegas has shut its all-night marriage license office. [. . .] The sacredness that formerly characterized weddings was exploited by the entertainment industry in hosting TV weddings, with gifts, free honeymoon, etc., and spectacular coverage. Audiences seem to like this. Then, too, couples who enjoy publicity started a trend toward getting married while skydiving or scuba diving, or engaging in any activity that was outlandish enough to raise an eyebrow. At this point, all one can predict is that silver and golden wedding anniversaries will become increasingly rare.[2]

The closure of Las Vegas' all-night marriage license office seems more boon than blight for the prospects of future marriages, though certainly, the article does make some observations that seem valid. Divorce is more common than it once was, cohabitation as an alternative to marriage has increased,[3] and many Americans would likely agree that the media and entertainment industries are not always supportive of marriage.

But if some of the observations are valid, the article's conclusions seem to accept the notion that marriage is a risky venture. To accept, as Kreyche does, that "silver and golden wedding anniversaries will become increasingly rare" is to accept the bleak future for marriage. The question, of course, is whether such opinions are accurate, and what the real state of marriage is in the United States.

When former Vice President Al Gore and his wife, Tipper, announced their divorce after four decades of marriage, it wasn't the usual celebrity divorce. The Gores had been married far beyond the "seven year itch" and had made it onto the list of long-married celebrities.[4] In 2002, Al and Tipper had even coauthored a book on family and marriage titled *Joined at the Heart: The Transformation of the American Family*. Their divorce could not be dismissed as mere tabloid material because they themselves had seemed to be not just a happy couple, but a stable couple.

Nevertheless, when the Gores divorced, many commentators did not seem surprised. After all, the common wisdom held, such an outcome wasn't unlikely. For many, the news story wasn't necessarily that the former vice president's marriage had failed—rather it was that the Gores were simply one of the half of all marriages that ended in divorce.

The lesson drawn from their divorce often seemed to be that this could happen to anyone—and that it *would* happen eventually to one in two married couples.

Discussing the break up, CNN noted that, "the U.S. Census estimates about half of marriages end in divorce, a sign that opting for divorce has become much more acceptable than the past when ending a marriage was taboo."[5]

The problem is that divorce is not nearly as likely an outcome as a successful marriage. In fact, marriage is far healthier than most people think in the one place that matters above all others: the homes of the American people.

Most Americans believe in their own marriages and in the institution of marriage in general. This is true despite the naysayers, the lack of respect for marriage sometimes evident in various films and television programs, and the degree of publicity surrounding the failure of high-profile marriages.

Though it might come as a shock to some, the vast majority of Americans will marry and the vast majority of those who are married say they are happy, giving our country a "living consensus" in favor of marriage.

That isn't to say that marriage—in people's lives, and in society at large—doesn't take its hits, or that marital stability is as high as it once was, but the situation is far better than we have been led to believe.

Unfortunately, the often-cited statistic that half of marriages end in divorce is based on the fact that the divorce rate is not properly understood, in part because crunching the numbers can be very complicated. As Dan Hurley wrote in a 2005 *New York Times* op-ed titled "Divorce Rate: It's Not as High as You Think":

> How many American marriages end in divorce? One in two, if you believe the statistic endlessly repeated in news media reports, academic papers and campaign speeches.
>
> The figure is based on a simple—and flawed—calculation: the annual marriage rate per 1,000 people compared with the annual divorce rate. In 2003, for example, the most recent year for which data is available, there were 7.5 marriages per 1,000 people and 3.8 divorces, according to the National Center for Health Statistics.
>
> But researchers say that this is misleading because the people who are divorcing in any given year are not the same as those who are marrying, and that the statistic is virtually useless in understanding divorce rates. In fact, they say, studies find that the divorce rate in the United States has never reached one in every two marriages, and new research suggests that, with rates now declining, it probably never will.[6]

Indeed, the most reliable statistics indicate that many more marriages succeed than fail. The Marriage Index—produced by the

National Marriage Project at the University of Virginia—estimates that more than 60 percent of first marriages are intact, and, along with many other sources, indicates that the divorce rate is falling.[7] In fact, since 1980, the number of divorces per 1,000 people has fallen steadily in the United States.[8]

Our own polling has likewise found that most married Americans have never experienced divorce. In fact, fewer than four in 10 Americans (37 percent) who have ever been married say they are currently—or have been—divorced, while 63 percent who walked down the aisle never divorced.[9]

That isn't always the story we hear—in some cases because the "fine print" warnings on the census data go unnoticed. For example, one 2007 *New York Times* article noted the divorce statistic is based on a census report indicating that "for the first time at least since World War II, women and men who married in the late 1970s had a less than even chance of still being married 25 years later" because of divorce, separation or being widowed.[10] But little more than a week after the census results were released, an op-ed by Betsey Stevenson and Justin Wolfers in *The New York Times* blew the whistle on some problems with this interpretation of the census report:

> But here's the rub: The census data came from a survey conducted in mid-2004, and at that time, it had not yet been 25 years since the wedding day of around 1 in 10 of those whose marriages they surveyed. And if your wedding was in late 1979, it was simply impossible to have celebrated a 25th anniversary when asked about your marriage in mid-2004. If the census survey had been conducted six months later, it would have found that a majority of those married in the second half of 1979 were happily moving into their 26th year of marriage. Once these marriages are added to the mix, it turns out that a majority of couples who tied the knot from 1975 to 1979—about 53 percent—reached their silver anniversary.

This surveying glitch affected only the most recent data. Still, factoring in an appropriate adjustment yields the conclusion that divorce rates have been falling, not rising. This is not just statistical smoke and mirrors: the Census Bureau warned that the most recent data understate the true stability of recent marriages. But a warning buried in a footnote does not always make the headlines."[11]

Divorce certainly affects those married in specific time periods more than others, but as Tara Parker Pope in her book *For Better: The Science of a Good Marriage* points out, there is cause for hope:

The divorce trends showing up in later generations are more hopeful. People married in the 1980s and 1990s are getting divorced at lower rates than their counterparts married in the 1970s. In fact, marital stability appears to be improving each decade.[12]

Stevenson and Wolfers also see a brighter future:

The story of ever-increasing divorce is a powerful narrative. It is also wrong. In fact, the divorce rate has been falling continuously over the past quarter-century, and is now at its lowest level since 1970. While marriage rates are also declining, those marriages that do occur are increasingly more stable.[13]

All of this is a far cry from what we usually hear about marriage, but it's the lived experience of the vast majority of Americans, most of whom get married, stay married, and say they are indeed living happily ever after—despite living in a country with the most liberal divorce laws in the Western world.[14]

Some have argued that a falling divorce rate isn't as important as people think, since, while divorce rates have fallen, so have marriage rates. Or as a *USA Today* headline put it in 2005 "Divorce declining, but so is marriage."[15] Again, as with the divorce rate, there is a lot more to the story, and we shouldn't necessarily assume that cohabitation is the primary cause of a decreased number of weddings in a given year.

First, as *The State of Our Unions* 2009, a report by the National Marriage Project, points out:

> Much of this decline—it is not clear just how much—results from the delaying of first marriages until older ages: the median age at first marriage went from 20 for females and 23 for males in 1960 to about 26 and 28, respectively, in 2007.[16]

Second, while the marriage rate has declined, we must exercise the same caution here as with divorce statistics. The current estimate given by *The State of Our Unions* in both 2005 and 2009 was in the 80-percent range, though they caution that the number will likely continue to slowly decline. As *USA Today* reported in June 2010, that range was confirmed by the CDC. It found that:

> Most Americans are likely to get married at some point in their lives, according to new federal data that show the probability of being married by age 40 is over 80 percent. For men, the likelihood of a first marriage by 40 is 81 percent; for women, it's 86 percent.[17]

There might be a slight decline in the percentage of people who ever marry, but the vast majority of every generation will be those who do.

Nor is this data overly skewed by "older" generations tending to be more traditional regarding marriage norms. In 2009, Child Trends research center polled 20- to 24-year-olds on their relationship status, values, attitudes and expectations, and found one in five had already married, and of those who were unmarried, 83 percent said marrying in the future was very important or important. Additionally, among those who were unmarried, there was great hope that they *would* get married in the next 10 years, with 70 percent saying they were "almost certain" or that they had "a good chance" of being married in the next 10 years. Of the rest, 20 percent think they have a 50-50 chance of getting married by then, and only 10 percent think they have slim chance.[18]

The fact that remaining unmarried has become less taboo doesn't mean that getting married has become unimportant. Less social pressure has not revealed that Americans have "outgrown" marriage, but rather that we have a persisting desire for it that goes beyond societal expectations.

Interestingly, the divorce rate may be falling even more in the economic crisis, as economic realities force couples to delay or rethink their divorce. According to a Princeton Survey Research Associates International poll commissioned by Bankrate, one-third of Americans said if they found themselves in an unhappy marriage, they would delay divorce because of tight finances.[19] For some, it could simply delay a divorce until later, as some commentators have pointed out[20]—or it could help some couples turn a corner, as was discussed in the recent *Newsweek* article "When Divorce Isn't the Only Choice."[21]

How marriage is discussed in public matters, and especially for those facing marital problems, the messages we transmit about marriage are vital. Whether or not the myth that "half of all marriages fail" is expedient politically or in some other way, its use should be abandoned—not only for its inaccuracy, but also for its effect. The harm done by the too-often repeated "statistic" was also discussed by Tara Parker-Pope. Beyond the numerical error, she notes that there are both private and public consequences of perpetuating the myth that half of marriages fail—consequences that can contribute to both the division of homes and the political divide.

For one thing, Parker-Pope wrote that inaccurate divorce statistics can undermine more marriages. It's a worthy concern. Speaking of her own marriage and divorce, she points out that she personally saw marriage as "a coin toss," and that she "was just among the unlucky 50 percent heading to court." Her conclusion from this: "Inflating divorce statistics has the potential to increase *everybody's* risk of getting divorced."[22]

While the resilience of Americans' marital success says a great deal about our national character and our ability to do well in spite of misguided statistical analysis, the constant stream of overly "high" divorce statistics can't be helpful—especially for those dealing with marital problems.

In fact, research suggests that for couples in a troubled marriage:

Two out of three unhappily married adults who avoided divorce or separation ended up considering themselves happily married five years later."[23] That is both a more accurate and more hopeful message for those working through marital issues. Those who are married need to hear the message that working things out usually *can* lead to "happily ever after.

The team of researchers—led by Linda J. Waite of the University of Chicago—studied data from the National Survey of Families and Households. Among their surprising findings was that "unhappily married adults who divorced or separated were no happier, on average, than unhappily married adults who stayed married. Even unhappy spouses who had divorced and remarried were no happier, on average. than unhappy spouses who stayed married."[24]

Many surveys have actually found that marriage is a key component in happiness. Looking back at its past three years' worth of data on Americans' happiness, Gallup has even suggested that one's marital state may be a stronger indicator of happiness than the amount of his or her annual salary. Married people at any income level were as likely—if not more likely—to report being happy than the wealthiest unmarried people.[25]

Figure 1: Happiness in Marriage

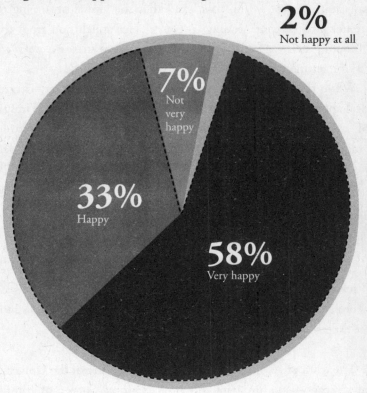

2%
Not happy at all

7%
Not
very
happy

33%
Happy

58%
Very happy

Are you very happy, happy, not very happy or not happy at all in your marriage?

The Knights of Columbus/Marist Poll July 2010 Survey

The numbers are astounding. Our polling in July 2010—in the midst of the recession with all the added economic stress—found that 91 percent of married Americans were either very happy (58 percent) or happy (33 percent) with their marriages.

A recent Marist poll also found that 19 out of 20 married Americans (95 percent) believe they married the right person.[26] Understandably, younger respondents (ages 18 to 29) are more likely to say they "found the right one"—in fact, 100 percent say this. But lest people dismiss this merely as the "honeymoon stage," keep in mind that in no age group did fewer than 92 percent of people say they had married the right person.[27]

A *CBS News* poll found something similar: Nine in 10 married Americans say that if they had to choose again, they would still marry their spouse.[28]

But 11 out of 12 married Americans are happy, with all the common misconceptions about marriage that exist in this country, it is entirely possible that many of those couples think they are part of the lucky "half," rather than the majority. There are many reasons that this misconception exists, but it's time for us to make choices and policies based on facts. There should be more care in the way marriage is portrayed, reported on or legislated about, and that care should be based on the true state of married households—united (and likely to stay that way).

The mythology surrounding marriage and divorce has an effect on other political debates. Parker-Pope noted that the 50 percent divorce statistic is widespread in part because it can support a variety of political viewpoints—a sort of "political Swiss Army knife, handy for any number of agendas," as *Time* magazine's review of her book put it.[29] Parker-Pope points out that skewed data is also used at times by those who see a place for non-traditional relationships, believing that humans have "outgrown" the institution of marriage.[30]

Misleading statistics and the idea that marriage is somehow passé help no one, least of all those living in difficult marriages.

Regardless of the ease of using a 50 percent statistic, or its political efficacy, or its status based on the opinion that "everyone knows" it's true. The repetition of so-called data—skewed by misunderstanding—is not helpful to our national conversation about marriage. It is also not helpful to those considering marriage, or in a difficult marriage, and it is far out of step with what most Americans experience in their own marriages. With divorce rates falling, it's far out of step with the future of marriages, too.

We shouldn't give up on the institution of marriage, though we should abandon the use of misleading and incorrect statistics.

Not only is the divorce rate lower than is commonly believed—and falling—but consistent with this, Americans strongly oppose marital infidelity. In our polling, nine out of 10 describe "having an affair" as morally wrong.[31]

Of course, given the way marriage statistics are commonly misunderstood and misused, it's no surprise that Americans think marriage is undervalued. What is surprising and hopeful is that about three-quarters of us—of all ages—haven't lost heart, but instead actually think it should be valued more.

On another aspect of our national conversation on marriage, the statistics used have also been seen as more evenly split than they actually are. The conventional wisdom—apparently made more credible by some polling, media reports and political debates—is that the country is split down the middle on the issue of same-sex marriage. A *CBS News* headline characterizes the public debate: "Poll: Americans Divided on Gay Marriage."[32] As with the abortion issue, the slightest change in the percentages is seen as a distinct advantage for one of the two "opposite" positions.

As with marriage numbers in general, there is much more to it than that. Just as Americans—in their lives and values—are not nearly as divided by divorce as we have been led to believe, the same holds true on the issue of same-sex marriage.

Our polling has found that when three options are given—same-sex marriage, civil unions, or no legal recognition—there is actually a nationwide consensus against redefining marriage. Twenty-eight percent of Americans support civil unions, while 38 percent favor no legal recognition for same-sex couples.[33]

In other words, nearly seven in 10 Americans do not favor same-sex marriage.

This was confirmed in a *CBS News* poll as well, which found that "although six in 10 Americans think some form of legal recognition is appropriate for same-sex couples, only a third of Americans think those couples should be allowed to marry."[34] That's not a 50-50 split, it's a consensus.

Certainly, this is a more nuanced view than is usually presented. Though when a poll seems to indicate the slightest shift, it's big news.[35] It's worth looking beyond the strictly "support" or "don't support" numbers and noting that a majority of Americans continue to question the morality of same-sex marriage, with 54 percent believing it is "morally wrong."[36] Of course, Americans can disagree on an issue and still respect the people they disagree with. A recent Fox News/Opinion Dynamics Poll found that a consensus of 67 percent believes that religious Americans are very (22 percent)

Table 1: Spectrum of Opinion on Same-Sex Marriage

Which comes closer to your view:	
Gay and lesbian couples should be allowed to legally marry	34%
Gay and lesbian couples should be allowed to legally form civil unions, but not marry	28%
There should be no legal recognition of the relationship between gay and lesbian couples	38%

The Knights of Columbus/Marist Poll July 2010 Survey

or somewhat (45 percent) tolerant of gays and lesbians. Less than a third thought that they were somewhat intolerant (14 percent) or very intolerant (14 percent).[37]

Rejecting a respectful debate or resorting to pejorative labels to describe those who disagree on this issue is not constructive. The American people are both tolerant of diversity and simultaneously cautious about redefining so fundamental an institution as marriage. That's the consensus.

Most Americans debating marriage are personally invested in the issue, and emotions can run high. The discussion should continue with this in mind, and with an understanding that the key issue for most Americans is what marriage is, has been, and should be in the future. When considering an issue of such magnitude, Americans want to think carefully about the effects of changing the way we define marriage, opening it up to relationships never before included in its definition.

Americans also want political representatives who share their beliefs in this area. Our polling found that supporting marriage "only between a man and a woman" was one of only four positions out of 20 that most Americans said would lead them to "definitely vote" for a candidate. The vast majority—71 percent—said they either would definitely vote for a candidate holding that position (51 percent), or would vote for him or her with reservations (20 percent). Less than a third (29 percent) said they definitely would not vote for such a candidate.[38]

These numbers make clear why Americans have voted to define marriage in the traditional sense in all 31 states where the people have voted on this issue. Equally interesting is the fact that in those places where marriage has been redefined (Massachusetts, Vermont, Connecticut, New Hampshire, Iowa, the District of Columbia and California), it was done so by judges or legislators, not by public vote.

Americans today, as in the past, tend to move cautiously when debating issues of great importance. Writing on the process of the American political system, Alexis de Tocqueville observed:

> What one understands by republic in the United States is the slow and tranquil action of society on itself. It is a regular state really founded on the enlightened will of the people. It is a conciliating government, in which resolutions ripen for a long time, are discussed slowly and executed only when mature.[39]

The American people are in the midst of a conversation on the future of marriage. It is a conversation with significant implications, and it elicits strong emotions on both sides. But it is a conversation that ought to be both civil and fully thought out.

In a manner that is respectful to all sides, Americans at every level should learn the lesson of *Roe v. Wade*: Precipitous judicial action that attempts to foreclose public discourse ensures a legacy of contentious controversy. Such an outcome in the marriage debate, without the moral force of the American people behind it, would be much more divisive than our current national conversation about marriage.

While the American people are discussing the definition of marriage, they also have a lot to say about what they think of divorce. It might seem puzzling that a country whose people think about, discuss and value marriage so much has, at the same time, some of the most liberal divorce laws in the Western world.[40] In fact, our polling has found most Americans, 64 percent, favor the "no-fault" divorce, such as one granted solely for irreconcilable differences, over divorce only for a serious reason, 36 percent.[41] The numbers are almost exactly the same as the number of those Americans who have ever been married but not divorced, 63 percent, and those who have been divorced, 37 percent.[42]

We could speculate as to any number of reasons why Americans might prefer "no-fault" divorce laws. Whatever the reasons, however, the majority of married Americans don't have much interest in getting a divorce themselves, and even those who do divorce still believe in the institution of marriage. A GfK Roper poll commissioned by the online community divorce360.com found that more than 80 percent of divorced Americans still strongly believe in the institution of marriage. Conversely, only seven percent of women say they no longer believe in marriage, and an even smaller percentage of men—three percent—say the same.[43]

The same poll showed that 85 percent of people who have considered divorcing their spouse are open to efforts to save the marriage, including 58 percent who say they are willing to seek help through marriage therapy.[44]

Wanting to leave "no-fault" divorce on the books doesn't mean that Americans want to get a divorce, nor does it mean they think that divorce is without its problems—especially where children are concerned.

Our polling found that nearly two-thirds of Americans (64 percent) believe that divorce creates more problems than it solves, especially when children are involved. By more than five to one (66 percent to 13 percent), a consensus thinks that parents divorcing is a negative thing for children in the long-term.[45]

Again, the sense of the vast majority of the American people is quite accurate. Social science research has shown profound negative effects from divorce, especially on children.

The data is devastating. Judith Wallerstein and Joan Kelley observed in their five-year study of divorced families, *Surviving the Breakup*, that following their parents' divorce, "two-thirds of the children, especially the younger children, yearned for the absent parent . . . with an intensity (which the researchers described as) profoundly moving."[46]

Five years after the divorce, 37 percent of the children were

Figure 2: Opinion on Divorce

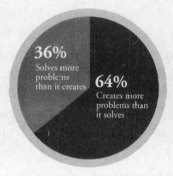
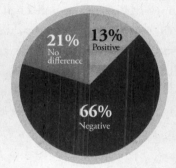

In general, do you think divorce, especially when children are involved, creates more problems than it solves or solves more problems than it creates?

Overall, in most cases, do you think when parents divorce, it is a positive thing or a negative thing for children in the long term, or does it make no difference?

The Knights of Columbus/Marist Poll, July 2010 Survey

moderately to severely depressed, intensely unhappy and dissatisfied with their lives, and their unhappiness was greater at five years than it had been at one and a half years after the divorce. Ten years after the divorce 41 percent of the children were "underachieving, self-deprecating and sometimes angry young men and women."[47]

Elizabeth Marquardt, herself a child of divorce, conducted a study of more than 1,500 children from divorced homes and wrote about her findings and some of the stories of the individual children in her 2005 book *Between Two Worlds*. She writes:

> *This is the truth about us:* Some of us, many more than those from intact families, struggle with serious problems. Our parents' divorce is linked to our higher rates of depression, suicidal attempts and thoughts, health problems, childhood sexual abuse, school dropout, failure to attend college, arrests, addiction, teen pregnancy, and more. Some of us were practically abandoned to raise ourselves in the wake of our parents' divorce and turned to drugs or alcohol or thrill seeking to numb our pain. Some of us were abused by new adults who came into the house when one of our parents left. Some of us continue to struggle with the scars left from our parents' divorce: we have a harder time finishing school, getting and keeping jobs, maintaining relationships, and having lasting marriages. We end up living on the margins, struggling with our pain, while our friends and neighbors move on with their lives . . . Yet those who are visibly suffering are the tip of the iceberg.[48]

In our polling, we asked adults who had experienced divorce as children to pick the word that best describes how they felt when told of their parents' divorce. More than three-quarters say they had a negative reaction, feeling either "confused" (34 percent), "sad" (29 percent), "angry" (9 percent), or "guilty" (4 percent). By contrast, less than a quarter had a positive response, with positive emotions all polling in the single digits: "relieved" (9 percent), "hopeful" (7 percent), and "happy" (3 percent).[49]

Such reactions are consistent with the studies done by Wallerstein and Kelly, in which they noted:

> . . . Only a few of the children in our study thought their parents were happily married, yet the overwhelming majority preferred the unhappy marriage to the divorce. As the children spoke with us, we found that although many of them had lived for years in an unhappy home, they did not experience the divorce as a solution to their unhappiness, nor did they greet it with relief at the time, or for several years thereafter. Many of the children, despite the unhappiness of their parents, were in fact relatively happy and considered their situation neither better nor worse than that of other families around them. They would, in fact, have been content to hobble along. The divorce was a bolt of lightning that struck them when they had not even been aware of the existence of a storm.[50]

Americans' concern about the effects of divorce on children is consistent with the research. For instance, Elizabeth Marquardt has found:

> While a 'good divorce' is better than a bad divorce, it is still not good. . . . For no matter how amicable divorced parents might be and how much they love each other and care for the child [. . .] their willingness to do these things does absolutely nothing to diminish the radical restructuring of the child's universe.[51]

Immersed in a culture that has tasted for itself the bitter fruits of divorce and broken families, Americans already seem to know what many studies have also shown: Divorce is not the marital outcome anyone dreams of going into a marriage, and it hits children particularly hard. Despite the acceptance of divorce in society and law, we as a people are honest about its tragic effects—and we long for an American society that treasures marriage even more.

That's what the numbers tell us everywhere we look. In every generation since the 19th century, 90 percent of American women have married, and today the estimated number is almost as high.[52]

Of Americans who are married, more than nine in 10 are "very happy" or "happy." Marriage is both the top "life goal" for Americans and something—along with respect for other people and personal responsibility—that tops the list of what Americans think should be valued even more in our society. This perspective is not limited only to older generations. In fact, among Millennials, concern that marriage is undervalued was at the top of the list, ahead of worries that too little value was placed on personal responsibility, respect for others, honesty and integrity, concern for the less fortunate, tolerance of people who are different, respect for the law, a work ethic, belief in God, and religious observance.[53]

Those numbers make even more sense when we stop to consider that the vast majority of young people plan to marry.[54]

There is strong support for marriage—not just in the numbers, but in the daily lives of most Americans.

Those who would use marriage cynically—whether for political advantage, for a laugh or for a headline—should remember what Dr. Beau Weston had to say about a poll that found that most Americans who were married were happy: "In general, most people marry and have kids. Normally, the happiest people in society are married parents. They are most economically productive. They are really the pillars and backbone in society."[55]

That's a far cry from what we often hear about marriage, but it's the experience, of the vast majority of Americans. Despite the mythologized divorce rate and the other hurdles that marriage sometimes faces in the way that it's portrayed, most Americans get married, stay married, and *do* live happily ever after.

For most, marriage is a success story—and successful marriages are here to stay.

Beyond Red and Blue: What We Can Do for Our Country

In February 2009, as the financial crisis was widening, the Knights of Columbus organized the *Neighbors Helping Neighbors* summit on volunteerism in New York City, bringing together volunteer organizations, charities, religious groups, educational institutions, the media and business. All of us came together to ask a question suggested almost 50 years ago by President John F. Kennedy in his inaugural address. We wanted to know not what our country could do for us, but what we could do for our country—for our fellow Americans in need.

More than 150 attendees from scores of organizations around the country discussed the issues facing our fellow Americans and ways that each and every one of us could—and truly must—help. Shortly before the summit, a number of reports had indicated that charitable giving was down because of the recession. In response, the Knights of Columbus, as an organization with nearly 130 years of experience in volunteer service, suggested that other groups interested in helping those in need in their communities should consider the powerful effect volunteering can have. We wanted to make the point that people might not have money in a recession, but they do have time, and that time donated to a worthy cause can make a profound difference.

In early 2009, we knew Americans were generous. We had seen it with Knights of Columbus members who had donated more than 626 million hours to charity in the preceding decade and almost 68 million hours in 2008 alone. We knew from experience that many Americans were willing both to give a dollar and to lend a helping hand. However, what we didn't know then—but know now—was just how many Americans are willing to act as their brother's keeper.

Our polling almost a year later revealed that two-thirds of Americans both volunteer their time and donate money to charity.[1] But when Americans do good for our country and for our neighbors, it isn't done self-consciously.

As we have found repeatedly in our polling, giving people flexibility in their answer choices paints a much more realistic picture on many issues than simply asking yes or no questions.

For example, when we asked Americans only if they had volunteered without providing a list of volunteer activities, only a little over a third responded that they had (34 percent).[2] This doesn't mean Americans don't volunteer; it means they engage in many activities we would classify as volunteering, but which they don't necessarily see as extraordinary.

This has long been the case. As he traveled across the newly formed American nation in the 1800s, French essayist Alexis de Tocqueville was fascinated by what he called American "associations"—groups that today would certainly include many of our country's charitable and volunteer organizations. He observed that such associations did everything—from building seminaries and churches to creating hospitals and schools, to distributing books and supporting missionaries.[3] These associations, Tocqueville noted, were unique to America, and "there is nothing," he argued, "that deserves more to attract our regard."[4]

As *New York Times* columnist Nicholas Kristof discussed in December 2008, Americans are head and shoulders above their European counterparts in terms of individual charitable donations:

European countries seem to show more compassion than America in providing safety nets for the poor, and they give far more humanitarian foreign aid per capita than the United States does. But as individuals, Europeans are far less charitable than Americans. Americans give sums to charity equivalent to 1.67 percent of G.N.P. . . . The British are second, with 0.73 percent, while the stingiest people on the list are the French, at 0.14 percent.[5]

Giving from our own pockets and of our own time is one thing that defines us as Americans.

What the polling shows is that we are a people who are simultaneously self-reliant and ready to give to those in need. We give back, but expect our personal choices to be the key to our own success.[6] About two-thirds of us don't expect help from our neighbors when times are tough,[7] but two-thirds of us give money to charity and volunteer.

As we've seen throughout this book, the faith of Americans in most of their institutions has been shaken, but they see two groups as moving the moral compass of our nation in the right direction far more than anyone else: volunteers and charitable organizations. In fact, those two groups were the only ones that more than six in 10 Americans thought were having a positive influence on the moral compass—73 percent for volunteers and 61 percent for charitable organizations.[8]

Those who "do for their country," those who give their time for the common good, are the people Americans respect most.

Sadly, while Americans have the most respect for those who serve the public—our volunteers—they least respect the moral leadership of public servants—our politicians.

In fact, 81 percent of Americans say that politicians are moving the moral compass in the wrong direction.[9] There is no shortage of reasons for this opinion. There is the hyper-partisan nature of politics not shared by the American people, the constant news of political scandals and, of course, the political debates more often filled with slogans and name-calling than with civil discussion about the needs of our country.

As Ronald Brownstein has pointed out:

> The reflexive, even ritualized, combat of modern politics leaves fewer and fewer attractive choices for all Americans who don't want to be conscripted into a battle between feuding ideologues. . . . [10]

Things are so divided in the "battle between feuding ideologues," that perhaps we need to look at advice from a time when the world seemed as divided as our political parties today. At the height of the Cold War, President Kennedy's inaugural discussed the need for civility between nations at odds. Those in the overly polarized halls of government—locked in the battle of red versus blue—might well heed his words today:

> So let us begin anew—remembering on both sides that civility is not a sign of weakness, and sincerity is always subject to proof. Let us never negotiate out of fear. But let us never fear to negotiate.
>
> Let both sides explore what problems unite us instead of belaboring those problems which divide us. [11]

That's what Americans are looking for. We wonder whatever happened to those like Jimmy Stewart's character, Mr. Smith, in the Frank Capra-Myles Connolly political classic *Mr. Smith Goes to Washington*. We want elected officials like Mr. Smith. We think honorable public servants can exist in Washington—not only in films about Washington. Two-thirds of us (66 percent) believe one can be successful in politics and remain ethical. [12] But almost as many Americans don't think this happens very often. More than six in 10 Americans (62 percent) rate politicians as having a poor level of honesty and ethical conduct. Just one percent said "excellent," and "excellent" and "good" combined came to only eight percent.[13]

It seems undeniable that there is a values gap between the American people and those in, and closest to, the government. As we have discussed, 62 percent of Americans believe family values are very important, while less than a quarter of Beltway insiders feel that way.[14]

Most Americans see other, formerly vaunted institutions as almost as out of touch with us as our elected officials. It's not just in Washington that Americans are looking for the likes of *Mr. Smith*, it's in Hollywood too. Almost three-quarters of Americans say that the entertainment industry is moving the moral compass in the wrong direction (73 percent).[15]

Entertainment researcher and commentator Ted Baehr has gone so far as to attribute the decline of network television viewership in some part to the explosion of profanity and sexual content of TV programming—not exactly fare that is "family values" friendly. There is at least some good news for those looking for more ethical entertainment though. Baehr points out that the movie industry waned when it got away from moral principles, but has remained economically viable by serving up more family friendly fare lately.[16]

As is true in business in general, it seems that one can be "ethical and successful" in the entertainment industry. According to media critic Michael Medved:

There has been a series of studies confirming that research, showing that the R rating is in fact a commercial *disadvantage*. The result of all of these studies has been a de-emphasis on that rating and a higher percentage of PG and PG-13 films. In fact, it has become common, and it never was before, that filmmakers—as part of their contract—have to promise that they will avoid an R rating. So that's the good news, that there's a spreading recognition that people do not really crave harsh language and graphic sexuality and violence.[17]

This isn't to say that both TV and movies are always "values" friendly, but perhaps things are beginning to trend in the right direction in Hollywood—to the benefit of both moviegoers and movie producers. We can hope that perhaps television programmers and other entertainers will learn Hollywood's lesson—if not for moral reasons, at least for economic ones.

Americans aren't necessarily looking for another Howard Beale (the fictional news anchor from the 1976 film *Network*), but they do want to change the moral channel when it comes to the media. They do want the truth. However, more than two-thirds of the American people (68 percent) say the media are pulling the moral compass in the wrong direction, and according to a Pew study in 2009, only 29 percent of Americans say that news organizations get the facts straight. And when the facts are misreported, there is a consensus among 70 percent of Americans that the media will try to cover up, rather than admit the errors.[18]

In addition, a Gallup study released in 2007 polled residents of 128 countries asking whether or not they had confidence in the quality and integrity of their media. Of the 128 countries surveyed, the U.S. media ranked 115th with only 32 percent of Americans feeling confident in their nation's media.[19] Only in five other countries did a greater percentage of people rank their media more negatively than the 66 percent of Americans who did so.

According to a Pew study in 2009, three out of every four Americans think that the press tends to favor one side over the other, regardless of what that side is.[20]

As Cal Thomas and Bob Beckel illustrate in their book *Common Ground*:

The polarization environment creates conflict, and conflict makes for prodigious amounts of press. The political media, which has its well-studied sets of biases, thrives on polarization. So, too, do the bottom feeders who promote conflict for profit and fame. These are the new kids on the block.[21]

If Americans aren't waiting for Beale, they are at least waiting for unbiased reporting, even if—like Beale—the media don't have all the answers.

The American people are looking for truth and values. That is not the typical solution presented by many of our institutions today.

The following were chosen from a broad list of business strategies sometimes undertaken during a crisis. One might notice that they also bear some resemblance to the sort of things we have been hearing from many of our institutions in terms of solving the problems facing us as a nation:

- Pin hopes on unproven strategies . . . often with much hype and fanfare.
- Make panicky, desperate moves in reaction to threats . . . draining cash and further eroding financial strength.
- Embark on a program of radical change or revolution, to transform or upend nearly every aspect of the company, jeopardizing or abandoning core strengths.
- Sell people on the promises of a brighter future to compensate for poor results.
- Destroy momentum with chronic restructuring and/or a series of inconsistent big decisions.
- Search for a leader-as-savior, with a bias for selecting a visionary from the outside who'll ride in and galvanize the company.[22]

This list is not a "to do" list, but the signs of what Jim Collins calls the fourth stage, or "Grasping for Salvation," along the path of the decline and fall of major corporations. It is the penultimate stage of collapse, right before the fifth stage known even more ominously as "Capitulation to Irrelevance or Death."[23]

While a valuable analysis for businesses seeking to pull themselves back from the brink, I think this list is even more valuable now as our nation faces a values gap between its people and its institutions, an economic crisis and a terribly divided political process.

More importantly, Collins's observations show not only that things can get worse if left unchecked, but also what needs to be done to initiate true recovery.

Now, despite the problems, I remain hopeful. And Collins, too, believes that even at stage four, recovery is possible. He states: "The path to recovery lies first and foremost in returning to sound management practices and rigorous strategic thinking."[24] This is done, he writes, by being "willing to form alliances with former adversaries, to accept necessary compromise, but never—ever—[by giving] up on your core values."[25]

By this measure, the American people have it right in terms of their proposed solutions to the problems facing our nation. In a population in which more than six in 10 see family values as very important, Americans—by more than three to one over any other choice—say "a return to traditional morals" is "the greatest hope for the future of the nation."[26]

Americans' instincts are correct. If we think of our nation as a business facing serious difficulties, then our core values—those present at our country's founding, present in President Kennedy's inaugural speech 50 years ago, and present today as the consensus of the American people—are indeed the way forward. These "family values" or "traditional morals" are indeed our country's best chance for moving forward and for recovering in our institutions

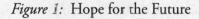

Figure 1: Hope for the Future

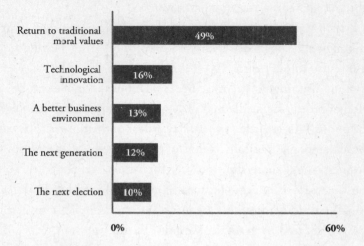

Return to traditional moral values — 49%

Technological innovation — 16%

A better business environment — 13%

The next generation — 12%

The next election — 10%

0%   60%

Which one of the following do you see is our greatest hope for the future of the nation?

The Knights of Columbus/Marist Poll July 2010 Survey

the values present in our homes, the values that have made this nation great.

It is time for us to look beyond the impasse on the political front, and to insist that those in politics see the hopeful unity—and the consensus concerning moral values—that we the people have achieved on the home front.

As discussed in the opening pages of this book, three Harris Polls conducted from 2008-2010, found that out of a list of 16 groups, only six were seen as having too little influence in Washington: churches and religious groups, racial minorities, opinion polls, nonprofit organizations, public opinion, and small business.[27]

Americans want institutions that share or reflect their values to take the lead in our political discussions, and certainly this seems like a more constructive option than the continuation of a political system crippled by excessive partisanship.

If such values can enter the realms of politics, economics, entertainment and the media, then, in the words of Vaclav Havel, "hope will return to our hearts."[28]

From Washington to Wall Street and from the movie studios of Hollywood to the media hub of New York, Americans are looking for nothing different than what they expect of themselves. The consensus among Americans is that one can be ethical in politics or business—and successful, too. On the whole, we don't believe in multiple sets of ethics—business ethics, media ethics, healthcare ethics, political ethics, etc. We just want ethics applied universally.

We must lead by example. We must be our brother's keeper, our neighbor's helper, an example for our civic, political and business leaders.

At his second inaugural, as the Civil War was coming to a close, President Abraham Lincoln said:

> With malice toward none; with charity for all; with firmness in the
> right, as God gives us to see the right, let us strive on to finish the
> work we are in; to bind up the nation's wounds; to care for him who
> shall have borne the battle, and for his widow, and his orphan—to do
> all which may achieve and cherish a just, and a lasting peace, among
> ourselves, and with all nations.[29]

Some have used this as a metaphor for what is needed to help heal our political system and our country today,[30] and that is certainly true. We are a people united by values, a people who respect most those who volunteer their time for others, and those organizations that facilitate such activity. We prefer altruism to power, and see morality as our best chance for a better future. The American people have achieved consensus—even in those places where we have been told we never could. Now we must lead. Now we must work so that our national conversations begin from our moral center, from our national concensus, not from edges or the fringes. It's not that we must bring a polarized American people together. We're not polarized. Rather, we must demand that the unity that already exists among Americans become the starting point for our national discussions.

A century after President Lincoln's words, Robert Kennedy said this when informed of the assassination of the Reverend Martin Luther King, Jr.:

> What we need in the United States is not division; what we need in the United States is not hatred; what we need in the United States is not violence or lawlessness; but is love and wisdom, and compassion toward one another, and a feeling of justice toward those who still suffer within our country whether they be white or black.[31]

Today this is truer than ever. While racial divisions have been improved, political divisions have not, and we might ask of our elected representatives to take this to heart—whether they be red or blue.

But it is not enough for us simply to ask. We must also act. And above all, we must give. We must become a nation in which the fact that two-thirds of us give money to charity and the same percentage give time is a good thing, but not good enough. We must approach every issue with charity, respect and civility, realizing that our consensus on moral values allows us to find consensus even on the most contentious issues of our day.

Fifty years later, it is time—"with malice toward none and charity towards all"—for us to answer again the call that captures the values of the vast majority of the American people, and can rebuild those "pillars of support"[32] so fundamental to our nation and to its future.

It is the final statement that President Kennedy made in his inaugural address:

> With a good conscience our only sure reward, with history the final judge of our deeds let us go forth to lead the land we love, asking His blessing and His help, but knowing that here on earth God's work must truly be our own.[33]

Notes

A word about our polls: In 2008, the Knights of Columbus was pleased to launch our Moral Compass project with the Marist Institute for Public Opinion. In the years since, we've had the pleasure of working with Marist on new surveys, exploring new topics. Most are cited in this book. For more information on all of our polling, including more detailed results and tables, please visit www.kofc.org/moralcompass.

CHAPTER I
BEYOND A HOUSE DIVIDED: OUR MORAL COMPASS

1. *Network*. Screenplay by Paddy Chayefsky (Dir. Sidney Lumet, Perf. William Holden, United Artists, 1976).

2. John McCormick and Catherine Dodge, "Americans Disapproving Obama May Enable Republican Gains," *Bloomberg* (July 15, 2010. Accessed July 25, 2010. www.bloomberg.com/news/2010-07-14/americans-disappoving-of-obama-policies-poised-to-enable-republican-gains.html).

3. Frank I. Luntz, *What Americans Really Want . . . Really: the Truth about Our Hopes, Dreams, and Fears* (New York: Hyperion, 2009), Appendix, "What Americans Really Want . . . Really Survey Results," Question 1, 276.

4. Jim Collins, *How the Mighty Fall and Why Some Companies Never Give In* (New York: HarperCollins, 2009), 81.

5. Knights of Columbus/Marist Poll July 2010 Survey.

6. Ronald Brownstein, *The Second Civil War: How Extreme Partisanship Has Paralyzed Washington and Polarized America* (New York: Penguin, 2007).

7. George Washington, "Farewell Address" (*Daily American Advertiser* [Philadelphia] September 19, 1796. Available from the Avalon Project, Yale Law School, Lillian Goldman Law Library. Accessed July, 2010. avalon.law.yale.edu/18th_century/washing.asp).

8. Harris Interactive, "Business Divides: Big Companies Have Too Much Power and Influence in D.C., Small Business Has Too Little," Dir. Regina A. Corso (April 1, 2010. Accessed July 26, 2010. Survey Conducted February 16-21, 2010. www.harrisinteractive.com/NewsRoom/HarrisPolls/tabid/447/mid/1508/articleId/115/ctl/ReadCustom%20Default/Default.aspx, Table 1).

9. Ibid.

10. Ibid.

11. Knights of Columbus/Marist Poll July 2010 Survey.

12. Knights of Columbus/Marist Poll January 2010 Survey.

13. Knights of Columbus/Marist Poll July 2010 Survey.

14. Knights of Columbus/Marist Poll January 2010 Survey.

15. Ibid. 7.

16. Abraham Lincoln, "Gettysburg Address" (Gettysburg, Pennsylvania, Thursday, November 19, 1863. Available from the Avalon Project, Yale Law School, Lillian Goldman Law Library. Accessed July, 2010. avalon.law.yale.edu/19th_century/gettyb.asp).

17. Martin Luther King Jr., "Letter from a Birmingham Jail" (Birmingham, Alabama, April 16, 1963. Available from the African Studies Center of the University of Pennsylvania. Accessed July, 2010. www.africa.upenn.edu/Articles_Gen/Letter_Birmingham.html).

18. Knights of Columbus/Marist Poll January 2010 Survey.

19. Alan Wolfe, *Moral Freedom: the Search for Virtue in a World of Choice* (New York: W.W. Norton, 2002), 195.

20. Knights of Columbus/Marist Poll January 2010 Survey.

21. Ibid.

22. Ibid.

23. Abraham Lincoln, "First Inaugural Address" (Washington D.C. March 4, 1861. Available from the Avalon Project, Yale Law School, Lillian Goldman Law Library. Accessed August 17, 2010. avalon.law.yale.edu/19th_ century/lincoln1.asp).

24. Abraham Lincoln, "Second Inaugural Address" (Washington D.C. March 4, 1865. Available from the Avalon Project, Yale Law School, Lillian Goldman Law Library. Accessed July, 2010. avalon.law.yale.edu/19th_century/lincoln2.asp).

25. Knights of Columbus/Marist Poll July 2010 Survey.

Chapter 2
Beyond the Wall of Separation: Religion in America

1. George Washington, "Farewell Address," (1796, available from the Avalon Project, Yale Law School, Lillian Goldman Law Library. Accessed July 27, 2010. avalon.law.yale.edu/18th_century/washing.asp).

2. Alexis de Tocqueville, *Democracy in America*, trans. by Harvey Mansfield and Delba Winthrop (London: University of Chicago Press, 2000), 282.

3. Jon Meacham, "The End of Christian America" *Newsweek* (April 4, 2009. Accessed July 26, 2010. www.newsweek.com/2009/04/03/the-end-of-christian-america.html).

4. Knights of Columbus/Marist Poll April 2009 Survey

5. Meacham, "The End of Christian America."

6. Knights of Columbus/Marist Poll January 2010 Survey.

7. Knights of Columbus/Marist Poll July 2010 Survey.

8. Knights of Columbus/Marist Poll January 2010 Survey.

9. Ibid.

10. Knights of Columbus/Marist Poll January 2010 Survey.

11. Knights of Columbus/Marist Poll July 2010 Survey.

12. Knights of Columbus/Marist Poll January 2010 Survey.

13. *Gallup*, "Religion," (2009, Accessed July 26, 2010, www.gallup.com/poll/1690/religion.aspx).

14. *The World Values Survey* (2005-2008 Wave, Accessed July 26, 2010, www.wvsevsdb.com/wvs/WVSAnalize.jsp). Selected countries/samples: *Cyprus [2006], Finland [2005], France [2006], Germany [2006], Great Britain [2006], Italy [2005], Netherlands [2006], Poland [2005], Slovenia [2005], Spain [2007], Sweden [2006].*

15. Knights of Columbus/Marist Poll January 2010 Survey.

16. Knights of Columbus/Marist Poll July 2010 Survey.

17. Ibid.

18. *Rasmussen Reports*, "National Day of Prayer," April 21-22, 2010 (Accessed July 26, 2010. www.rasmussenreports.com/premium_content/econ_cross tabs/april_2010/crosstabs_national_day_of_prayer_april_21_22_2010).

19. Ibid.

20. David G. Savage, "Supreme Court Says Mojave Cross Can Stand," *The Los Angeles Times* (April 29, 2010. Accessed July 27, 2010. http://articles.la-times.com/2010/apr/29/nation/la-na-court-mojave-cross-20100429).

21. *Rasmussen Reports*, "Religious Symbols," December 8, 2009 (Accessed July 27, 2010. www.rasmussenreports.com/premium_content/econ_crosstabs/december_2009/crosstabs_religious_symbols_december_8_2009).

22. *Rasmussen Reports*, "National Day of Prayer."

23. Ibid.

24. Ibid.

25. Ibid.

26. *Rasmussen Reports*, "Religious Symbols."

27. *Rasmussen Reports*, "Pledge of Allegiance," November 22-23, 2008 (Accessed July 27, 2010. www.rasmussenreports.com/premium_content/ political_tracking_crosstabs/november_2008/crosstabs_pledge_of_ allegiance_november_22_23_2008).

28. Knights of Columbus/Marist Poll July 2010 Survey.

29. *Wallace v. Jaffree*, 472 U.S. 38 (1985. Accessed July 25, 2010. http://supreme.justia.com/us/472/38/case.html).

30. Ibid.

31. Thomas Jefferson, "Letter to the Danbury Baptists," (Jan. 1, 1802. Available from the Library of Congress. Accessed July 27, 2010, www.loc.gov/loc/lcib/9806/danpost.html).

32. Thomas Jefferson, "Second Inaugural Address," (March 4, 1805. Available from the Avalon Project, Yale Law School, Lillian Goldman Law Library. Accessed July 27, 2010. avalon.law.yale.edu/19th_century/jefinau2.asp).

33. Tocqueville, 280.

34. *Constitution of the United States* (Available from the United States Senate. Accessed July 27, 2010. www.senate.gov/civics/constitution_item/consti-tution.htm).

35. John F. Kennedy, "Address to Protestant Ministers," (Sept. 12, 1960. Available from *NPR*. Accessed July 27, 2010.www.npr.org/templates/story/ story.php?storyId=16920600).

36. John F. Kennedy, "Inaugural Address of John F. Kennedy," (Jan 20, 1961, Available from the Avalon Project, Yale Law School, Lillian Goldman Law Library. Accessed August 11, 2010. http://avalon.law.yale.edu/20th_cen-tury/kennedy.asp).

CHAPTER 3

BEYOND GREED: TOWARD MORALITY IN THE MARKETPLACE

1. Beth Healy and Casey Ross, "Citing 'Extraordinary Evil,' Judge Gives Madoff 150 Years in Prison," *The Boston Globe* (June 30, 2009. Accessed July 27, 2010. www.boston.com/business/articles/2009/06/30/citing_ 8216extraordinary_evil8217_judge_gives_madoff_150_years_in_prison/).

2. Suzy Jagger, "Madoff Whistleblower Harry Markopolos Says Securities and Exchange Commission Ignored His Warnings," *The Times* (Feb. 5,

2009. Accessed July 27, 2010. http://business.timesonline.co.uk/tol/business/industry_sectors/banking_and_finance/article5663759.ece).

3. Robert A. Sunshine, "The Budget and Economic Outlook: Fiscal Years 2009 to 2019," *Congressional Budget Office* (Jan. 8, 2009. Available from the *Committee on the Budget, United States Senate*. Accessed July 27, 2010. www.budget.senate.gov/democratic/testimony/2009/c1c8OutlookSunshineTestimony.pdf), 8.

4. "Distrust, Discontent, Anger and Partisan Rancor." *The Pew Research Center for the People and the Press* (April 18, 2010. Accessed July 27, 2010. http://people-press.org/report/606/trust-in-government).

5. Frank I. Luntz, *What Americans Really Want . . . Really: The Truth About Our Hopes, Dreams, and Fears* (New York: Hyperion, 2009), Appendix, "What Americans Really Want . . . Really Survey Results," Question 26, 283.

6. Knights of Columbus/Marist Poll July 2010 Survey.

7. *Wall Street*, Screenplay by Stanley Weiser (Dir. Oliver Stone, Perf. Michael Douglas. *Twentieth Century Fox Film Corporation*, 1987).

8. " . . . from Washington to Wall Street, too often a different attitude prevailed. Wealth was valued over work, selfishness over sacrifice, greed over responsibility." from Barack Obama, "Remarks by the President at AFL-CIO Labor Day Picnic," (September 7, 2009. Available from *The White House, Office of the Press Secretary*. Accessed July 27, 2010. www.whitehouse.gov/the_press_office/Remarks-by-the-President-at-AFL-CIO-Labor-Day-Picnic).

9. "This foundation of our economy, the American worker, is strong but it has been put at risk by the greed and mismanagement of Wall Street and Washington." from John Bentley, "McCain: 'Greed of Wall Street' to Blame for Economic Meltdown," *CBS News* (Sept. 16, 2008. Accessed July 27, 2010. www.cbsnews.com/8301-502443_162-4452777-502443.html).

10. Oskari Juurikkala, "Greed Hurts: Causes of the Global Financial Crisis," *The Acton Institute* (Jan. 16, 2008. Accessed July 27, 2010. www.acton.org/commentary/425_greed_hurts.php).

11. Sally Steenland and Sarah Dreier, "It's a Moral Meltdown, Too," *Center for American Progress* (Oct. 7, 2008. Accessed July 27, 2010. www.americanprogress.org/issues/2008/10/moral_meltdown.html).

12. Michael Muskal, "GOP Calls for Bipartisan Approach On Financial Reform As Key Vote Nears," *The Los Angeles Times* (April 26, 2010. Accessed July 27, 2010. http://latimesblogs.latimes.com/dcnow/2010/04/gop-calls-for-bipartisan-approach-on-financial-reform-as-key-vote-nears.html).

13. David M. Herszenhorn, "Financial Reform Bill Limps Toward Vote," *The New York Times* (July 13, 2010. Accessed July 27, 2010. www.nytimes.com/2010/07/14/business/14regulate.html).

14. Knights of Columbus/Marist Poll July 2010 Survey.

15. Knights of Columbus/Marist Poll July 2010 Survey.

16. Knights of Columbus/Marist Poll July 2010 Survey.

17. Knights of Columbus/Marist Poll January 2010 Survey and Knights of Columbus/Marist Poll July 2010 Survey.

18. Knights of Columbus/Marist Poll January 2010 Survey and Knights of Columbus/Marist Poll July 2010 Survey.

19. *Politico*, "Power and the People," July 9-14, 2010 (Accessed July 27, 2010, www.politico.com/static/PPM136_100718_poll_report.html).

20. Jagger, "Madoff Whistleblower Harry Markopolos Says Securities and Exchange Commission Ignored His Warnings."

21. Congress Urges Ouster of 2 Regulators," *The New York Times* (Nov. 23, 2004. Accessed July 28, 2010. www.nytimes.com/2004/11/23/business/23fannie.html?ref=armando_falcon_jr).

22. "The OFHEO Report: Allegations of Accounting and Management Failure at Fannie Mae," *U.S. House of Representatives, Subcommittee on Capital Markets, Insurance, and Government Sponsored Enterprises, Committee on Financial Services* (Oct. 6, 2004, Accessed July 28, 2010. http://commdocs.house.gov/committees/bank/hba97754.000/hba97754_of.htm), 15.

23. Eric Lipton, "Man Who Toppled Chief of Fannie Mae Is Seen as a David Who Beat Goliath," *The New York Times* (Dec. 23, 2004. Accessed July 28, 2010. www.nytimes.com/2004/12/23/business/23regs.html?_r=1&ref=armando_falcon_jr).

24. Corbett B. Daly, "Fannie, Freddie Regulator Sees Better Loan Quality," *Reuters* (July 21, 2010. Accessed July 28, 2010. www.reuters.com/article/idUSTRE66K6HD20100721).

25. *Milton Friedman on Donahue* 1979 (3/5). Interview between Milton Friedman and Phil Donahue (Excerpt from the Phil Donahue Show, 1979. Dir.

Ronald Weiner. Available on YouTube. Posted May 7, 2009. Accessed July 21, 2010. www.youtube.com/watch?v=GapXLpLoZBs).

26. Gary Galles, "Greed Label Used Sans Consistency." *Daily News* (Los Angeles) (May 10, 2006), N21.

27. "Rethinking Values in the Post-Crisis World," *World Economic Forum Annual Meeting 2010* (Jan 27, 2010. Accessed on July 28, 2010. Yunus, www.weforum.org/pdf/AM_2010/transcripts/rethinking-values.pdf).

28. Genesis 4:9 (New American Bible version).

29. Knights of Columbus/Marist Poll January 2010 Survey.

30. Joseph Cardinal Ratzinger, "Market, Economy and Ethics," *Acton Institute* (1985. Accessed July 28, 2010. www.acton.org/publications/occasionalpapers/publicat_occasionalpapers_ratzinger.php).

31. *Handbook of Economic and Ethics.* Edited by Jan Puiel and Irene van Staveren (Northampton (MA): Edward Elgar Publishers, 2009), 572-573. See Also: Athol Fitzgibbon, "Adam Smith's System of Liberty, Wealth, and Virtue: The Moral and Political Foundations of The Wealth of Nations." (New York: Oxford University Press, 1995).

32. Adam Smith, *Theory of Moral Sentiments* (London: George Bell and Sons, 1875), 436-437.

33. Knights of Columbus/Marist Poll January 2010 Survey.

34. Ibid.

35. Knights of Columbus/Marist Poll January 2009 Survey.

36. Knights of Columbus/Marist Poll July 2010 Survey.

37. Knights of Columbus/Marist Poll January 2009 Survey.

38. David Pitt, "Socially Responsible Investments Show Sustained Growth," *The Associated Press* (Aug. 8, 2010. Accessed August 9, 2010. www.boston .com/business/personalfinance/articles/2010/08/08/socially_responsible_ investments_show_sustained_growth/).

39. Jim Collins, *Built to Last* (New York: HarperCollins, 1994), Chapter 3 "More Than Profits."

40. Collins, 53.

41. "Automotive Industry Crisis," *The New York Times* (May 13, 2010. Accessed July 28, 2010. http://topics.nytimes.com/top/reference/times topics/subjects/c/credit_crisis/auto_industry/index.html).

42. Knights of Columbus/Marist Poll July 2010 Survey.

43. Knights of Columbus/Marist Poll January 2009 Survey.

44. Falcon, 10.

45. Vaclav Havel, "New Year's Address to the Nation," (Jan. 1, 1990. Accessed July 28, 2010. http://old.hrad.cz/president/Havel/speeches/1990/0101 _uk.html).

46. Francis Fukuyama, *The End of History and the Last Man* (New York: Free Press, 1992).

47. Knights of Columbus/Marist Poll January 2009 Survey.

Chapter 4
Beyond Partisan Politics: Values-based Leadership

1. "Partisan Politics," *Rasmussen Reports*, July 6-7, 2010 (Accessed August 14, 2010. www.rasmussenreports.com/public_content/politics/toplines/pt_ survey_toplines/july_2010/toplines_partisan_politics_july_6_7_2010).

2. Dana Blanton, "Fox News Poll: Voters Tired of Partisan Bickering, Loud Cell Phone Talker," *Fox News* (March 1, 2010, Survey Conducted Feb 23-24, 2010. Accessed August 14, 2010. www.foxnews.com/politics/2010/03/ 01/fox-news-poll-voters-tired-partisan-bickering-loud-cell-phone-talkers/).

3. Ronald Brownstein, *The Second Civil War: How Extreme Partisanship Has Paralyzed Washington and Polarized America* (New York: Penguin, 2007), 12.

4. Browstein, 12

5. David Gergen and Andy Zelleke, "America's other deficit: leadership," *Christian Science Monitor* (October 22, 2008.) 9.

6. Cohen, Jon and Philip Ruckner, "Poll Finds Most Americans Are Unhappy with Government," *Washington Post* (February 11, 2010. Survey Conducted February 4-8, 2010. www.washingtonpost.com/wp-srv/politics/polls/postpoll_021010.html?sid=ST2010021100035).

7. Ibid. Question 40.

8. Lydia Saad, *Gallup*, "Congress Ranks Last in Confidence in Institutions," (Survey Conducted July 8-11. Accessed July 22, 2010. www.gallup.com/poll/141512/Congress-Ranks-Last-Confidence-Institutions.aspx)

9. Jeff Jones and Lydia Saad, Gallup, "Gallup Poll Social Series: Consumption Habits," (July 22, 2010. Survey Conducted July 8-11, 2010. Accessed

July 2010. Topline Data for Question 7, www.gallup.com/poll/File/141515/Confidence_Institutions_July_22_2010.pdf) 2.

10. Knights of Columbus/Marist Poll July 2010 Survey.

11. Ibid.

12. Ibid.

13. Politico Poll, "Power and the People," (July 19, 2010. Survey Conducted July 9—14 by Penn Schoen Berland. Accessed July 26, 2010. www.politico.com/static/PPM136_100718_poll_report.html).

14. Ibid.

15. Ibid.

16. Ibid.

17. Knights of Columbus/Marist Poll July 2010 Survey.

18. Jeffrey Jones, "Renewed Desire for U.S. Gov't to Promote Traditional Values," *Gallup* (Sep 29, 2009. Survey Conducted Aug 31—Sep 9, 2009. Accessed August 14, 2010. www.gallup.com/poll/123326/renewed-desire-gov-promote-traditional-values.aspx).

19. Jeffrey Jones, "Americans' Outlook for U.S. Morality Remains Bleak," *Gallup* (May 17, 2010. Survey Conducted May 3-6, 2010. Accessed August 14, 2010. www.gallup.com/poll/128042/Americans-Outlook-Morality-Remains-Bleak.aspx).

20. Sean Theirault, "The Case of the Vanishing Moderates." (2003, Available from *Michigan State University*. Accessed August 17 2010. www.msu.edu/~rchde/Theriault.pdf).

21. "About the Third Way," Democratic Leadership Council. (June 1, 1998. Accessed June, 2010. www.dlc.org/ndol_ci.cfm?kaid=128&subid=187&contentid=895).

22. CNN/USA Today/Gallup, "Poll: Nation Split on Bush as Uniter or Divider," *CNN.com* January 19, 2005. (Accessed July, 2010. Survey Conducted January 14—16, 2005. www.cnn.com/2005/ALLPOLITICS/01/19/poll/).

23. Wes Allison and Bill Adair, "Can Obama Keep promise of bipartisanship?" *St. Petersburg Times* (November 6, 2008. Accessed July, 2010. www.tampabay.com/news/politics/elections/article891974.ece)

24. Senate.gov, "Party Division in the Senate, 1789—Present" Available at

Senate.gov. Accessed July, 27, 2010. www.senate.gov/pagelayout/history/ one_item_and_teasers/partydiv.htm and House.gov, Office of the Clerk, "Party Divisions of the House of Representatives (1789 to Present)" Available at House.gov. Accessed July 27, 2010. clerk.house.gov/art_history/ house_history/partyDiv.html and Library of Congress, Prints and Photographs Reading Room, "Chronological List of Presidents, First Ladies, and Vice Presidents of the United States." Available at loc.gov. Accessed July 27, 2010. www.loc.gov/rr/print/list/057_chron.html.

25. Thomas Jefferson, "A Summary View of the Rights of British America" (Available from the Avalon Project, Yale Law School, Lillian Goldman Law Library. Accessed August 14, 2010. http://avalon.law.yale.edu/18th_century/jeffsumm.asp).

26. Abraham Lincoln, "Gettysburg Address" (Gettysburg, Pennsylvania, Thursday, November 19, 1863. Available from the Avalon Project, Yale Law School, Lillian Goldman Law Library. Accessed July, 2010. avalon.law.yale.edu/19th_century/gettyb.asp).

27. John F. Kennedy, "First Inaugural Address" (Washington, D.C., January 20, 1961. Available from the American Presidency Project. Accessed July, 2010. www.presidency.ucsb.edu/ws/index.php?pid=8032).

28. Martin Luther King Jr., "Letter from a Birmingham Jail" (Birmingham, Alabama, April 16, 1963. Available from the African Studies Center of the University of Pennsylvania. Accessed July, 2010. www.africa.upenn.edu/Articles_Gen/Letter_Birmingham.html).

29. Knights of Columbus/Marist Poll July 2010 Survey.

30. Ronald Reagan, "First Inaugural Address," (January 20, 1981. Accessed July 27, 2010. Available from the Avalon Project, Yale Law School, Lillian Goldman Law Library. http://avalon.law.yale.edu/20th_century/reagan1.asp)

31. *AP–National Constitution Center Poll* (September 15, 2009. Survey Conducted September 3—September 8, 2009. Accessed July 20, 2010. http://surveys.ap.org/data/GfK/AP-GfK%20Poll%20Constitution%20 Topline%20with%20trends%20final%20091109.pdf).

32. Knights of Columbus-Marist, "July," 106.

33. *Rasmussen Reports*, "23% Say U.S. Government Has Consent of the Governed" (July 16, 2009. Survey Conducted July 12-14, 2010. Accessed July,

2010. www.rasmussenreports.com/public_content/politics/general_poli-tics/july_2010/23_say_u_s_government_has_the_consent_of_the_gov-erned).

34. Ibid.

35. Knights of Columbus/Marist Poll January 2010 Survey.

36. *Quinnipiac University*, "More U.S. Voters Want Arizona-Like Immigration Law, Quinnipiac University National Poll Finds; Support for Offshore Drilling Drops" (June 1, 2010. Survey Conducted May 19-24, 2010. Accessed August 14, 2010. www.quinnipiac.edu/x1295.xml?ReleaseID=1460).

37. For Arizona polls, see the collection at www.pollingreport.com/immigra-tion.htm, including: *Fox News/Opinion Dynamics Poll* dated July 27-28, 2010. *CNN/Opinion Research Corporation Poll* dated July 16-21, 2010; *ABC News/Washington Post Poll* dated June 3-6, 2010; etc. For polls on the need for immigration reform: *Pew Research/National Journal Congressional Connection Poll* (Survey Conducted Jul 8-11, 2010. Accessed August 14, 2010. Available from www.pollingreport.com/immigration.htm).

38. *America's Voice*, "Bipartisan Poll: In Arizona Aftermath, Public Demands National Immigration Reform" (Survey Conducted May 13-19, 2010. Accessed August 14, 2010. http://americasvoiceonline.org/index.php/polling/entry/bipartisan_poll_in_arizona_aftermath_public_demands_na tional_immigrati).

39. Knights of Columbus/Marist Poll July 2010 Survey.

40. *Quinnipiac University*, "More U.S. Voters Want Arizona-Like Immigration Law, Quinnipiac University National Poll Finds; Support for Offshore Drilling Drops."

41. Knights of Columbus/Marist Poll July 2010 Survey.

42. *Washington Post/ABC News Poll*, "Washington Post-ABC News Poll" (Sur-vey Conducted July 7-11, 2010. Accessed August 14, 2010. www.washing-tonpost.com/wp-srv/politics/polls/postpoll_07132010.html).

43. Knights of Columbus/Marist Poll January 2010 Survey.

44. Knights of Columbus/Marist Poll July 2010 Survey.

45. Ibid.

46. Ibid.

47. Jeffrey M. Jones, Gallup, "Big Gov't Still Viewed as Greater Threat Than

Big Business." (April 20, 2009. Accessed July, 2010. Survey Conducted March 27-29, 2009. www.gallup.com/poll/117739/Big-Gov-Viewed-Greater-Threat-Big-Business.aspx).

48. AP –National Constitution Center Poll.

49. *Rasmussen Reports*, "70% Say Big Government and Big Business on the Same Team," April 23, 2009. (Accessed July 26, 2010. www.rasmussenreports.com/public_content/business/general_business/april_2009/70_say_big_government_and_big_business_on_the_same_team).

50. *Rasmussen Reports*, "Health Care Law: 58% Favor Repeal, But 48% Says It's Unlikely," July 26, 2010 (Accessed July 26, 2010. Survey Conducted July 24-25, 2010. www.rasmussenreports.com/public_content/politics/current_events/healthcare/health_care_law).

51. Ibid.

52. Stephanie Condon. "Support for Health Care Drops." *CBS News*. July 13, 2010. (Accessed July, 2010. Survey Conducted July 9-12, 2010. www.cbsnews.com/8301-503544_162-20010453-503544.html?tag=contentMain;contentBody).

53. Knights of Columbus/Marist Poll July 2010 Survey.

54. Daniel Callahan, *Setting Limits: Medical Goals in an Aging Society.* (Washington, D.C.: Georgetown UP, 1995).

55. Knights of Columbus/Marist Poll July 2010 Survey.

56. Ibid.

57. Ibid.

58. Ibid.

59. George Washington, "Farewell Address," (1796, available from the Avalon Project, Yale Law School, Lillian Goldman Law Library. Accessed July 27, 2010. avalon.law.yale.edu/18th_century/washing.asp).

60. Alexis de Tocqueville, *Democracy in America.* Trans. Mansfield, Harvey and Winthrop, Delba. University of Chicago Press: London 2000. 282.

61. Knights of Columbus/Marist Poll July 2010 Survey.

62. Ibid.

63. Ibid.

64. Ibid.

65. Knights of Columbus/Marist Poll January 2010 Survey.

66. Knights of Columbus/Marist Poll July 2010 Survey.

CHAPTER 5

BEYOND THE CLASH OF ABSOLUTES: ABORTION

1. Laurence H. Tribe, *Abortion: The Clash of Absolutes* (New York: Norton, 1992), 6.

2. George W. Bush, Speech to the Republican National Convention, August 3, 2000 (Accessed July 26, 2010 from www.ontheissues.org/George_W_Bush_Abortion.htm).

3. Barack H. Obama, "Remarks by the President in Commencement Address at the University of Notre Dame" South Bend, IN, May 17, 2009 (The White House, Office of the Press Secretary. Accessed July 26, 2010 www.whitehouse.gov/the_press_office/Remarks-by-the-President-at-Notre-Dame-Commencement/).

4. John Zogby, *The Way We'll Be: The Zogby Report on the Transformation of the American Dream* (New York: Random House, 2008), 53.

5. Tribe, 8.

6. *Gallup*, "The New Normal on Abortion: Americans More 'Pro-Life,'" May 14, 2009 (Survey Conducted May 3-6, 2010. Accessed July 28, 2010. www.gallup.com/poll/128036/new-normal-abortion-americans-pro-life.aspx?version=print).

7. Laurie Goodstein, "Support Appears to Drop for Abortion Rights," *The New York Times* (Oct. 1, 2009. Accessed July 28, 2010. www.nytimes.com/2009/10/02/us/02abortion.html).

8. Dan Gilgoff, "Gallup Poll: Americans Evenly Split on Abortion Between 'Pro-Life' and 'Pro-Choice,'" *U.S. News & World Report* (Aug. 7, 2009. Accessed July 28, 2010. http://politics.usnews.com/news/blogs/god-and-country/2009/08/07/gallup-poll-americans-evenly-split-on-abortion-between-pro-life-and-pro-choice.html).

9. *Gallup*, "The New Normal on Abortion."

10. Ibid.

11. Knights of Columbus/Marist Poll "Abortion in America" Survey.

12. Knights of Columbus/Marist Poll July 2010 Survey.

13. Ibid.

14. Ibid.

15. *CNN/Opinion Research Corporation Poll*, November 13-15, 2009 (Available

from *The Polling Report*. Accessed August 11, 2001. www.pollingreport .com/abortion2.htm).

16. Knights of Columbus/Marist Poll July 2010 Survey.

17. Ibid.

18. Agostino Bono. "Survey shows high school seniors feel abortion is wrong, favor curbs," Catholic News Service. Jan. 12, 2006.

19. John Zogby, *The Way We'll Be: The Zogby report on the Transformation of the American Dream* (New York: Random House, 2008), 104.

20. Sarah Kiff, "Remember Roe!: How can the next generation defend abortion rights when they don't think abortion rights need defending?," *Newsweek* (April 16, 2010. Accessed August 11, 2010. www.newsweek .com/2010/04/15/remember-roe.html).

21. Knights of Columbus/Marist Poll January 2010 Survey.

22. *Hamilton College*, "Hot Button Issues Poll: Guns, Gays, and Abortion," January 2006 (Accessed August 14, 2010. www.hamilton.edu/news/ polls/HotButtonFinalReport.pdf).

23. Dennis Gilbert, "Hamilton College Hot Button Issues Poll: Guns, Gays, And Abortion," *Hamilton College* (Survey Conducted November 10-20, 2005. Accessed August 11, 2010. www.hamilton.edu/news/polls/hotbut- tonissues/analysis.html).

24. Based on the abortion ratio (abortions per 1000 live births) for 16 year olds and for 17 year olds, 2005, From Sonya B. Gamble, Lilo T. Strauss, et. al., "Abortion Surveillance—United States, 2005" *The Center for Disease Control and Prevention* (Nov. 28, 2008. Accessed August 11, 2010, www.cdc.gov/mmwr/preview/mmwrhtml/ss5713a1.htm#tab5), Table 5.

25. "State Facts About Abortion: New York," *Guttmacher Institute* (Accessed August 15, 2010. www.guttmacher.org/pubs/sfaa/new_york.html).

26. Knights of Columbus/Marist Poll "Abortion in America" Survey.

27. Ibid.

28. Knights of Columbus/Marist Poll July 2010 Survey.

29. Ibid.

30. *CNN*, "Poll: Majority Favor Abortion Funding Ban," Nov. 18, 2009 (Survey Conducted Nov. 13-15, 2009. Accessed July 28, 2010. www.cnn.com/ 2009/POLITICS/11/18/abortion.poll/).

31. Zogby, 103.

32. "State Policies in Brief: As of August 1, 2010." Guttmacher Institute (Accessed August 15, 2010. www.guttmacher.org/statecenter/spibs/spib_OAL.pdf).

33. *Roe v. Wade*, 410 U.S. 179 (1973).

34. Ibid., 192.

35. Ramesh Ponnuru, *The Party of Death: The Democrats, the Media, The Courts, and the Disregard for Human Life* (Washington D.C.: Regnery Publishing 2006),10.

36. Jennifer Greenstein Altmann, "Her husband bakes, Scalia sings: Ginsburg describes the lighter side of the Supreme Court," *Princeton University* (October 23, 2008. Accessed August 11, 2010. www.princeton.edu/main/news/archive/S22/48/08A80/).

37. Clarke Forsythe, *Politics for the Greatest Good: The Case for Prudence in the Public Square* (Downers Grove (IL): InterVarsity Press, 2009), 183.

38. John Hart Ely, "The Wages of Crying Wolf," *The Yale Law Journal* (1973. Available in *The Human Life Review, Vol. 1*. New York: The Human Life Foundation. 1975), 52-60.

39. Mary Ann Glendon, *Abortion and Divorce in Western Law: American Failures, European Challenges* (Cambridge: Harvard University Press, 1987), 2.

40. Joseph Carroll, "Race and Education 50 Years After Brown v. Board of Education," *Gallup* (May 14, 2004. Accessed July 28, 2010. www.gallup.com/poll/11686/race-education-years-after-brown-board-education.aspx).

41. Louis Harris, "Majority Favors Abortion," *The Harris Survey* (May 26, 1975. Accessed August 10, 2010. www.harrisinteractive.com/vault/Harris-Interactive-Poll-Research-MAJORITY-FAVORS-ABORTION-1975-05.pdf).

42. Carl Anderson, *A Civilization of Love* (New York: Harper Collins. 2008), 128.

43. Knights of Columbus/Marist Poll July 2010 Survey.

44. Knights of Columbus/Marist Poll "Abortion in America" Survey.

45. Martin Luther King, Jr., "Letter From A Birmingham Jail," (Apr. 16, 1963. Available from the African Studies Center, University of Pennsylvania.

Accessed July 28, 2010.www.africa.upenn.edu/Articles_Gen/Letter_Birmingham.html).

Chapter 6
Beyond Mythology: The Statistics of Marriage

1. Jessica Bennet and Jesse Ellison, "'I Don't': The Case Against Marriage," *Newsweek* (June 11, 2010. Accessed July 26, 2010. www.newsweek.com/2010/06/11/i-don-t.html).

2. Gerald F. Kreyche "The Demise of Marriage." *USA Today* (Available from BNET, FindArticles.com. Accessed August 14, 2010. http:// findarticles.com/p/articles/mi_m1272/is_2740_135/ai_n17134360/).

3. Betsy Hart, "Weddings becoming less common, but . . . ; Married couples more likely to be happy than those just living together," *Chicago Sun Times*, (March 11, 2010, B6).

4. For example, Smart Marriages website's list of long-married couples. (Accessed August 14, 2010. www.smartmarriages.com/long.married.celebrity.couples.html).

5. Stephenie Chen, "Why Call It Quits After Decades of Marriage?," *CNN* (June 2, 2010. Accessed July 26, 2010. www.cnn.com/2010/LIVING/06/02/al.gore.separation.40years.marriage/index.html).

6. Dan Hurley, "Divorce Rate: It's Not As High As You Think," *New York Times* (April 19, 2005. Accessed July 26, 2010, www.nytimes.com/2005/04/19/health/19divo.html).

7. "The Marriage Index: A Proposal to Establish Leading Marriage Indicators," *Institute for American Values* (2009, Accessed July 26, 2010, www.americanvalues.org/pdfs/IAV_Marriage_Index_09_25_09.pdf).

8. Barbara Kantrowitz, "When Divorce Isn't the Only Choice," *Newsweek* (March 29, 2010, Accessed July 26, 2010, www.newsweek.com/2010/03/28/when-divorce-isn-t-the-only-choice.html). See also www.virginia.edu/marriageproject/pdfs/Union_ 11_25_09.pdf figure 3, p. 43. Accessed August 14, 2010.

9. Knights of Columbus/Marist Poll July 2010 Survey.

10. Sam Roberts, "25th Anniversary Mark Elusive for Many Couples," *New York Times* (Sept. 20, 2007, A14).

11. Betsey Stevenson and Justin Wolfers, "Divorced from Reality," *New York Times* (Sept. 29, 2007, A15).

12. Tara Parker-Pope, *For Better: The Science of a Good Marriage* (New York: Dutton, 2010), 12.

13. Stevenson and Wolfers, "Divorced from Reality."

14. See: Mary Ann Glendon, *Abortion and Divorce in Western Law: American Failures, European Challenges* (Cambridge: Harvard University Press, 1987).

15. Sharon Jayson, "Divorce Declining, But So Is Marriage" *USA Today* (July 18, 2005, Accessed July 26, 2010, www.usatoday.com/news/nation/2005-07-18-cohabit-divorce_x.htm).

16. "The State of Our Unions: Marriage in America 2009," *The National Marriage Project and Institute for American Values*, ed. W. Bradford Wilcox, (December 2009, Accessed July 26, 2010, www.virginia.edu/marriageproject/pdfs/Union_11_25_09.pdf), 68.

17. Sharon Jayson, "Chance of Marrying by 40? Over 80%, CDC Says," *USA Today* (June 30, 2009, Accessed July 26, 2010, www.usatoday.com/news/health/2009-06-30-cdcmarriage_odds_N.htm).

18. Mindy Scott, Erin Schelar, et. al., "Young Adults Attitudes About Relationships and Marriage: Times May Have Changed, But Expectations Remain High." *Child Trends* Research Brief (July 2009. Accessed August 15, 2010. www.childtrends.org/Files//Child_Trends-2009_07_08_RB_YoungAdultAttitudes.pdf).

19. Sheyna Steiner, "Poll: 92% Say Home Is A Good Investment," *Bankrate* (Accessed August 15, 2010. www.bankrate.com/finance/financial-literacy/poll-americans-fret-about-family-finances-1.aspx).

20. For example, see: Gabrielle Boston, "Couples Delay Divorce, Wait Out Recession," *The Washington Times* (Nov. 22, 2009. Accessed August 15, 2010. www.washingtontimes.com/news/2009/nov/22/couples-delaying-divorce-wait-out-recession/).

21. Kantrowitz, "When Divorce Isn't The Only Choice."

22. Pope, 15.

23. Linda J. Waite, Don Browning, et. al., "Does Divorce Make People Happy?: Findings From a Study of Unhappy Marriages," *Institute for*

American Values (2002, Accessed July 26, 2010, www.americanvalues.org/html/does_divorce_make_people_happy.html).

24. Ibid.

25. *Gallup*, "More Than Half of Americans 'Very Satisfied' with Personal Life," January 3, 2007. (Survey Conducted Dec. 11-14, 2006. Accessed July 26, 2010. www.gallup.com/poll/26032/more-than-half-americans-very-satisfied-personal-life.aspx).

26. *Marist Poll*, "Do you thin you married the right person, or not?" (Accessed August 15, 2010. http://maristpoll.marist.edu/wp-content/misc/usapolls/US100617/Marriage_Soul%20Mates/Married_Right_Person.htm).

27. *Marist Poll*, "Do you think you married the right person, or not?"

28. *CBS News*, "Love and Marriage," January 29-31, 2010. Accessed August 15, 2010. www.cbsnews.com/htdocs/pdf/Poll_Jan10dLove.pdf?tag=contentMain;contentBody).

29. Belinda Luscombe, "Are Marriage Statistics Divorced From Reality," Time (May 24, 2010, Accessed July 26, 2010, www.time.com/time/magazine/article/0,9171,1989124,00.html).

30. Tara Parker-Pope, *For Better: The Science of a Good Marriage*, 15-16.

31. Knights of Columbus/Marist Poll January 2010 Survey.

32. *CBS News*, "Poll: Americans Divided on Gay Marriage," April 3, 2009. (Survey Conducted March 12-16, 2009. Accessed July 26, 2010, www.cbsnews.com/8301-503544_162-4917681-503544.html).

33. Knights of Columbus/Marist Poll July 2010 Survey.

34. *CBS News*, "Poll: Americans Divided on Gay Marriage."

35. *CNN/Opinion Research*, "Americans split evenly on gay marriage," (Aug 11, 2010. Accessed August 15, 2010. http://politicalticker.blogs.cnn.com/2010/08/11/americans-split-evenly-on-gay-marriage/).

36. Knights of Columbus/Marist Poll January 2010 Survey.

37. *Fox News/Opinion Dynamics* "Where Americans Stand on the Issues," May 18, 2009 (Accessed August 15, 2010. www.foxnews.com/projects/pdf/051809_issues_web.pdf).

38. Knights of Columbus/Marist Poll July 2010 Survey.

39. Alexis de Tocqueville, *Democracy in America*, trans. by Harvey Mansfield and Delba Winthrop (London: University of Chicago Press, 2000), 379-380.

40. Mary Ann Glendon, *Abortion and Divorce in Western Law: American Failures, European Challenges* (Cambridge: Harvard University Press, 1987), 64.

41. Knights of Columbus/Marist Poll July 2010 Survey.

42. Ibid.

43. Michele Kimball, "Poll: Great Faith in Marriage," *Divorce360.com* (Accessed July 26, 2010, www.divorce360.com/divorce-articles/statistics/us/poll-great-faith-in-marriage.aspx?artid=255).

44. Michele Kimball, "Poll: Most Work to Save Marriage," *Divorce360.com* (Accessed July 26, 2010, www.divorce360.com/divorce-articles/counseling/save-marriage/poll-most-work-to-save-marriage.aspx?artid=278).

45. Knights of Columbus/Marist Poll July 2010 Survey.

46. Judith Wallerstein and Joan Kelly, *Surviving the Breakup: How Children and Parents Cope with Divorce* (New York: Basic Books, 1980), 46.

47. Judith Wallerstein and Sandra Blakeslee, *Second Chances: Men, Women and Children a Decade After Divorce* (New York: Ticknor and Fields, 1989), 299 See also: Judith Wallerstein and Joan Kelly, Surviving the Breakup: How Children and Parents Cope with Divorce (New York: Basic Books, 1980).

48. Elizabeth Marquardt, *Between Two Worlds* (New York: Crown, 2005), 188-9.

49. Knights of Columbus/Marist Poll July 2010 Survey.

50. Ibid., 10-11.

51. Ibid., 16.

52. "The State of Our Unions: Marriage in America 2009," 69.

53. Knights of Columbus/Marist Poll January 2010 Survey.

54. Mindy Scott, Erin Schelar, et. al., "Young Adults Attitudes About Relationships and Marriage: Times May Have Changed, but Expectations Remain High."

55. Michele Kimball, "Poll: Most Marriages Are Happy."

CHAPTER 7

BEYOND RED AND BLUE: WHAT WE CAN DO FOR OUR COUNTRY

1. Knights of Columbus/Marist Poll January 2010 Survey.

2. Knights of Columbus/Marist Poll July 2010 Survey.

3. Alexis de Tocqueville, *Democracy in America*, trans. by Harvey Mansfield and Delba Winthrop (London: University of Chicago Press, 2000), 489-492.

4. Scott Rasmussen likewise cites de Tocqueville and the importance of American associations in making his case that the people are for self-governance at odds with our nation's governing elites in his book *In Search of Self-Governance* (Create Space: 2010), 4-5.

5. Nicholas Kristoff. "Bleeding Heart Tightwads." *The New York Times*. (December 20, 2008. Accessed August 15, 2010. http://www.nytimes.com/2008/12/21/opinion/21kristof.html?_r=1).

6. Knights of Columbus/Marist Poll July 2010 Survey.

7. Ibid.

8. Ibid.

9. Knights of Columbus/Marist Poll July 2010 Survey.

10. Ronald Brownstein, *The Second Civil War: How Extreme Partisanship Has Paralyzed Washington and Polarized America* (New York: Penguin, 2007), 13.

11. John F. Kennedy, "Inaugural Address of John F. Kennedy," (Jan 20, 1961, Available from the Avalon Project, Yale Law School, Lillian Goldman Law Library. Accessed August 11, 2010. http://avalon.law.yale.edu/20th_century/kennedy.asp).

12. Knights of Columbus/Marist Poll July 2010 Survey.

13. Ibid.

14. *Politico*, "Power and the People," July 9-14, 2010 (Accessed July 27, 2010, www.politico.com/static/PPM136_100718_poll_report.html).

15. Knights of Columbus/Marist Poll July 2010 Survey.

16. Ted Baehr, "Audiences Prefer Family-Friendly Movies with No Foul Language," *BigHollywood.com* (Accessed August 15, 2010. http://bighollywood.breitbart.com/drbaehr/2009/12/20/audiences-prefer-family-friendly-movies-with-no-foul-language/).

17. Jerold Aust, "Michael Medved on Media and the Family," *The Good News* (Accessed August 15, 2010. http://www.gnmagazine.org/issues/gn40/mediafamily.htm).

18. "Press Accuracy Rating Hits Two Decade Low." *The Pew Research Center for People & the Press.* (September 13, 2009. Accessed August 15, 2010. http://people-press.org/report/543/).

19. Cynthia English, "Quality and Integrity of the World's Media Questioned." *Gallup* (December 17, 2007. Accessed August 15, 2010. http://www.gallup.com/poll/103300/quality-integrity-worlds-media-questioned.aspx).

20. "Press Accuracy Rating Hits Two Decade Low." *The Pew Research Center for People & the Press.*

21. Cal Thomas and Bob Beckel, *Common Ground: How to Stop the Partisan War that is Destroying America* (New York: Harper Collins. 2007), 43.

22. Jim Collins, *How the Mighty Fall and Why Some Companies Never Given In,* (New York: Harper Collins. 2009.), 90.

23. Ibid., Chapter 7: "Capitulation to Irrelevance or Death." 103-112.

24. Ibid., 117.

25. Ibid., 123.

26. KofC-Marist Poll, July 2010, Table 126.

27. Harris Interactive, "Business Divides: Big Companies Have Too Much Power and Influence in DC, Small Business Has Too Little", Dir. Regina A. Corso (April 1, 2010. Accessed July 26, 2010. Survey Conducted February 16-21, 2010. www.harrisinteractive.com/NewsRoom/HarrisPolls/tabid/447/mid/1508/articleId/115/ctl/ReadCustom%20Default/Default.aspx , Table 1.

28. Vaclav Havel, "New Year's Address to the Nation," (Jan. 1, 1990. Accessed July 28, 2010. http://old.hrad.cz/president/Havel/speeches/1990/0101_uk .html).

29. Abraham Lincoln, "Second Inaugural Address" (Washington D.C. March 4, 1865. Available from the Avalon Project, Yale Law School, Lillian Goldman Law Library. Accessed July, 2010. avalon law.yale.edu/19th_century/lincoln2.asp).

30. Ronald Brownstein, *The Second Civil War*, 416.

31. Robert F. Kennedy, "Remarks on the Assassination of Martin Luther King,

Jr." (April 4, 1968. Available from American Rhetoric. Accessed August 17, 2010. http://www.americanrhetoric.com/speeches/rfkonmlkdeath.html).

32. George Washington, "Farewell Address" (*Daily American Advertiser* [Philadelphia] September 19, 1796. Available from the Avalon Project, Yale Law School, Lillian Goldman Law Library. Accessed July, 2010. avalon.law.yale.edu/18th_century/washing.asp).

33. John F. Kennedy, "Inaugural Address of John F. Kennedy."